THE IRAN NUCLEAR DEAL

BY

Mr. Michael C. Enweren

And

DR. Michael C. Melvin

Contents

PREFACE

Joint Comprehensive Plan of Action (JCPOA) is an international agreement on the nuclear program of Iran signed in Vienna on 14 July 2015 between Iran, the P5+1 (the five permanent members of the United Nations Security Council—China, France, Russia, United Kingdom, United States and Germany) and the European Union. Formal negotiations toward the Joint Comprehensive Plan of Action on Iran's nuclear program began with the adoption of the Joint Plan of Action—an interim agreement on the Iranian nuclear program signed between Iran and the P5+1 countries in November 2013. For the next twenty months, Iran and the P5+1 countries engaged in negotiations, and in April 2015 agreed on a framework agreement for the final agreement. In July 2015, Iran and the P5+1 agreed on the Joint Comprehensive Plan of Action. Under the agreement, Iran agreed to eliminate its stockpile of medium-enriched uranium, cut its stockpile of low-enriched uranium by 98%, and reduce by about two-thirds the number of its centrifuges for at least fifteen years. For the next fifteen years, Iran will only enrich uranium up to 3.67%. Iran also agreed not to build any new uranium-enriching or heavy-water facilities over the same period. Uranium-enrichment activities will be limited to a single facility using first-generation centrifuges for ten years. Other facilities will be converted to avoid proliferation risks. To monitor and verify Iran's compliance with the agreement, the International Atomic Energy Agency (IAEA) will have regular access to all Iranian nuclear facilities. The agreement provides that in return for verifiably abiding by its commitments, Iran will receive relief from U.S., European Union, and United Nations Security Council nuclear-related sanctions.

CHAPTER ONE

Introduction

A nuclear weapon uses a fissile material to cause a nuclear chain reaction. The most commonly used materials have been uranium 235 (U-235) and plutonium 239 (P-239). Both uranium 233 (U-233) and reactor-grade plutonium have also been used. The amount of uranium or plutonium needed depends on the sophistication of the design, with a simple design requiring approximately 15 kg of uranium or 6 kg of plutonium and a sophisticated design requiring as little as 9 kg of uranium or 2 kg of plutonium. Plutonium is almost nonexistent in nature, and natural uranium is about 99.3% uranium 238 (U-238) and 0.7% U-235. Therefore, to make a weapon, either uranium must be enriched, or plutonium must be produced. Uranium enrichment is also frequently necessary for nuclear power. For this reason, uranium enrichment is a dual-use technology, a technology which "can be used both for civilian and for military purposes. Key strategies to prevent proliferation of nuclear arms include limiting the number of operating uranium enrichment plants and controlling the export of nuclear technology and fissile material. Iranian development of nuclear technology began in the 1970s, when the U.S. Atoms for Peace program began providing assistance to Iran. Iran signed the Treaty on the Non-Proliferation of Nuclear Weapons (NPT) in 1968 as a non-nuclear weapons state and ratified the NPT in 1970.

In 1979, the Iranian Revolution took place, and Iran's nuclear program, which had developed some baseline capacity, fell to disarray as much of Iran's nuclear talent fled the country in the wake of the Revolution. And Iran engaged in a costly war with Iraq from 1980 to 1988. Starting in the later 1980s, Iran restarted its nuclear program, with assistance from Pakistan (which entered into a bilateral agreement with Iran in 1992), China (which did the same in 1990), and Russia (which did the same in 1992 and 1995).

Iran began pursuing an indigenous nuclear fuel cycle capability by developing a uranium mining infrastructure and experimenting with uranium conversion and enrichment. According to the nonpartisan Nuclear Threat Initiative, "*U.S. intelligence agencies have long suspected Iran of using its civilian nuclear program as a cover for clandestine weapons development.*" Iran, in contrast, "*has always insisted that its nuclear work is peaceful.*"

In August 2002, the Paris-based National Council of Resistance of Iran, an Iranian dissident group, publicly revealed the existence of two undeclared nuclear facilities, the Arak heavy-water production facility and the Natanz enrichment facility In February 2003, Iranian President Mohammad Khatami acknowledged the existence of the facilities and asserted that Iran had undertaken "small-scale enrichment experiments" to produce low-enriched uranium for nuclear power plants. In late February, International Atomic Energy Agency (IAEA) inspectors visited Natanz. In May 2003, Iran allowed IAEA inspectors to visit the Kalaye Electric Company, but refused to allow them to take samples, and an IAEA report the following month concluded that Iran had failed to meet its obligations under the previous agreement.

In June 2003, Iran faced with the prospect of being referred to the UN Security Council—entered into diplomatic negotiations with France, Germany, and the United Kingdom (the EU3). The U.S. refused to be involved in these negotiations.

In October 2003, the Tehran Declaration was reached between Iran and the EU 3; under this declaration Iran agreed to cooperate fully with the IAEA, sign the Additional Protocol. Temporarily Iran suspended all uranium enrichment. And in September and October 2003, the IAEA conducted several facility

In October 2003, the Tehran Declaration was reached

between Iran and the EU3; under this declaration Iran agreed to cooperate fully with the IAEA, sign the Additional Protocol. Temporarily Iran suspended all uranium enrichment. And in September and October 2003, the IAEA conducted several facility inspections. This was followed by the Paris Agreement in November 2004, in which Iran agreed to temporarily suspend enrichment and conversion activities, "including the manufacture, installation, testing, and operation of centrifuges, and committed to working with the EU-3 to find a mutually beneficial long-term diplomatic solution.

In August 2005, Mahmoud Ahmadinejad, a hard-liner, was elected president of Iran. He accused Iranian negotiators who had negotiated the Paris Accords of treason. Over the next two months, the EU 3 agreement fell apart as talks over the EU 3's proposed Long Term Agreement broke down; the Iranian government "felt that the proposal was heavy on demands, light on incentives, did not incorporate Iran's proposals, and violated the Paris Agreement." Iran notified the IAEA that it would resume uranium conversion at Esfahan.

In February 2006, Iran ended its voluntary implementation of the Additional Protocol and resumed enrichment at Natanz, prompting the IAEA Board of Governors to refer Iran to the UN Security Council. After the vote, Iran announced it would resume enrichment of uranium. In April 2006, Ahmadinejad announced that Iran had nuclear technology, but stated that it was purely for power generation and not for producing weapons. In June 2006, the EU 3 joined China, Russia, and the United States, to form the P5+1. The following month, July 2006, the UN Security Council its first resolution demanding Iran stops uranium enrichment and processing.

Altogether, from 2006 to 2010, the UN Security Council subsequently adopted six resolutions concerning Iran's nuclear program: 1696 (July 2006), 1737 (December 2006), 1747 (March 2007), 1803 (March 2008), 1835 (September 2008), and 1929 (June 2010). The legal authority for the IAEA Board of Governors referral

Altogether, from 2006 to 2010, the UN Security Council subsequently adopted six resolutions concerning Iran's nuclear program: 1696 (July 2006), 1737 (December 2006), 1747 (March 2007), 1803 (March 2008), 1835 (September 2008), and 1929 (June 2010). The legal authority for the IAEA Board of Governors referral and the Security Council resolutions was derived from the IAEA Statute and the United Nations Charter. The resolutions demanded that Iran cease enrichment activities and imposing sanctions on Iran, including bans on the transfer of nuclear and missile technology to the country and freezes on the assets of certain Iranian individuals and entities, in order to pressure the country.

However, in Resolution 1803 and elsewhere the Security Council also acknowledged Iran's rights under Article IV of the NPT, which provides for "the inalienable right ... to develop research, production and use of nuclear energy for peaceful Purposes." In July 2006, Iran opened the Arak heavy water production plant, which led to one of the Security Council resolutions. In September 2009, U.S. President Barack Obama, reveals the existence of an underground enrichment facility in Fordow, near Qom saying that "Iran's decision to build yet another nuclear facility without notifying the IAEA represents a direct challenge to the basic compact at the center of the non-proliferation regime." Israel threatened to take military action against Iran.

In a February 2007 interview with the Financial Times, IAEA director general Mohamed ElBaradei said that military action against Iran *"would be catastrophic, counterproductive"* and called for negotiations between the international community and Iran over the Iranian nuclear program. ElBaradei specifically proposed a *"double, simultaneous suspension, a time out as a confidence-building measure"*. Under which the international sanctions would be suspended and Iran would suspend enrichment. ElBaradei also said that *"if I look at it from a weapons perspective there are much more important issues to me than the suspension of enrichment]*," naming his top priorities as preventing Iran from *"going to industrial capacity until the issues are settled"; building confidence, with full inspection involving Iranian adoption of the Additional Protocol; and at all costs preventing Iran from moving out of the [treaty-based non-proliferation] system*."

A November 2007 U.S. National Intelligence Estimate assessed that Iran "*halted its nuclear weapons program*" in 2003; that estimate and subsequent U.S. Intelligence Community statements also assessed that the Iranian government at the time had was "*keeping open the 'option' to develop nuclear weapons" in the future*. A July 2015 Congressional Research Service report said that "*statements from the U.S. intelligence community indicate that Iran has the technological and industrial capacity to produce nuclear weapons at some point, but the U.S. government assesses that Tehran has not mastered all of the necessary technologies for building a nuclear weapon*."

In March 2013, the U.S. began a series of secret bilateral talks with Iranian officials in Oman, led by William Joseph Burns and Jake Sullivan on the American side and Ali Asghar Khaji on the Iranian side. In June 2013, Hassan Rouhani was elected president of Iran. Rouhani has been described as "*more moderate, pragmatic and willing to negotiate than Ahmadinejad*." However, in a 2006 nuclear negotiation with European powers, Rouhani said that Iran had used the negotiations to dupe the Europeans, saying that during the negotiations, Iran managed to master the conversion of uranium yellowcake at Isfahan, (the conversion of yellowcake is an important step in the nuclear fuel process). In August 2013, three days after his inauguration, Rouhani calls for a resumption of serious negotiations with the P5+1 on the Iranian nuclear program.

In September 2013, Obama and Rouhani had a telephone conversation, the first high-level contact between U.S. and Iranian leaders since 1979, and U.S.Secretary of State John Kerry had a meeting with Iranian foreign minister Mohammad Javad Zarif, signaling that the two countries had an opening to cooperation. After several rounds of negotiations, on 24 November 2013, the Joint Plan of Action, an interim agreement on the Iranian nuclear program, was signed between Iran and the P5+1 countries in Geneva, Switzerland. It consisted of a short-term freeze of portions of Iran's nuclear program in exchange for decreased economic sanctions on Iran, as the countries work towards a long-term agreement. The IAEA began "*more intrusive and frequent inspections*" under the interim agreement. The agreement was formally activated on 20 January 2014. On that day, the IAEA issued a report stating that Iran was adhering to the terms of the interim agreement, including stopping enrichment of uranium to 20 percent, beginning the dilution process (to reduce half of the stockpile of 20 percent enriched uranium to 3.5 percent), and halting work on the Arak heavy-water reactor. A major focus on the negotiations was limitations on Iran's key nuclear facilities: the Arak IR-40 heavy water reactor and production plant (which was under construction, but never became operational, as Iran agreed as part of the November 2013 Joint Plan of Action (interim agreement) not to commission or fuel the reactor); the Bushehr Nuclear Power Plant; the Gachin uranium mine; the Fordow Fuel Enrichment Plant; the Isfahan uranium-conversion plant; the Natanz uranium enrichment plant; and the Parchin military research and development complex.

Joint Comprehensive Plan of Action

The agreement between the P5+1+EU and Iran on the Joint Comprehensive Plan of Action (JCPOA) is the culmination of 20 months of "*arduous*" negotiations. The agreement followed the Joint Plan of Action (JPA), an interim agreement between the P5+1 powers and Iran that was agreed to on 24 November 2013 at Geneva. The Geneva agreement was an interim deal, in which Iran agreed to roll back parts of its nuclear program in exchange for relief from some sanctions. This went into effect on 20 January 2014. The parties agreed to extend their talks with a first extension deadline on 24 November 2014 and a second extension deadline set to 1 July 2015. An Iran nuclear deal framework was reached on 2 April 2015. Under this framework Iran agreed tentatively to accept restrictions on its nuclear program, all of which would last for at least a decade and some longer, and to submit to an increased intensity of international Inspections under a framework deal. These details were to be negotiated by the end of June 2015.

The negotiations toward a Joint Comprehensive Plan of Action were extended several times until the final agreement, the Joint Comprehensive Plan of Action, was finally reached on 14 July 2015. Subsequently the negotiations between Iran and the P5+1 continued. In April 2014, a framework deal was reached at Lausanne. Intense marathon negotiations then continued, with the last session in Vienna at the Palais Coburg lasting for seventeen days. At several points, negotiations appeared to be at risk of breaking down, but negotiators managed to come to agreement. As the negotiators neared a deal, U.S. Secretary of State John Kerry directly asked Iranian Foreign Minister Mohammad Javad Zarif to confirm that he was "*authorized to actually make a deal, not just by the [Iranian] president, but by the supreme leader?*" Zarif gave assurances that he was.

Ultimately, on 14 July 2015, all parties agreed to a landmark comprehensive nuclear agreement. At the time of the announcement, shortly before 11:00 GMT, the agreement was released to the public.

CHAPTER TWO

Content of the Joint Comprehensive Plan of Action

Preambles and general provisions for the deal as follows:

i. The Islamic Republic of Iran and the E3/EU+3 (China, France, Germany, the Russian Federation, the United Kingdom and the United States, with the High Representative of the European Union for Foreign Affairs and Security Policy) have decided upon this long-term Joint Comprehensive Plan of Action (JCPOA). This JCPOA, reflecting a step-by-step approach, includes the reciprocal commitments as laid down in this document and the annexes hereto and is to be endorsed by the United Nations (UN) Security Council.

ii. The full implementation of this JCPOA will ensure the exclusively peaceful nature of Iran's nuclear programme.

iii. Iran reaffirms that under no circumstances will Iran ever seek, develop or acquire any nuclear weapons.

iv. Successful implementation of this JCPOA will enable Iran to fully enjoy its right to nuclear energy for peaceful purposes under the relevant articles of the nuclear Non-Proliferation Treaty (NPT) in line with its obligations therein, and the Iranian nuclear programme will be treated in the same manner as that of any other non-nuclear-weapon state party to the NPT.

v. This JCPOA will produce the comprehensive lifting of all UN Security Council sanctions as well as multilateral and national sanctions related to Iran's nuclear programme, including steps on access in areas of trade, technology, finance and energy.

vi. The E3/EU+3 and Iran reaffirm their commitment to the purposes and principles of the United Nations as set out in the UN Charter.

vii. The E3/EU+3 and Iran acknowledge that the NPT remains the cornerstone of the nuclear non-proliferation regime and the essential foundation for the pursuit of nuclear disarmament and for the peaceful uses of nuclear energy.

viii. The E3/EU+3 and Iran commit to implement this JCPOA in good faith and in a constructive atmosphere, based on mutual respect, and to refrain from any action inconsistent with the letter, spirit and intent of this JCPOA that would undermine its successful implementation. The E3/EU+3 will refrain from imposing discriminatory regulatory and procedural requirements in lieu of the sanctions and restrictive measures covered by this JCPOA. This JCPOA builds on the implementation of the Joint Plan of Action (JPOA) agreed in Geneva on 24 November 2013.

ix. A Joint Commission consisting of the E3/EU+3 and Iran will be established to monitor the implementation of this JCPOA and will carry out the functions provided for in this JCPOA. This Joint Commission will address issues arising from the implementation of this JCPOA and will operate in accordance with the provisions as detailed in the relevant annex.

x. The International Atomic Energy Agency (IAEA) will be requested to monitor and verify the voluntary nuclear-related measures as detailed in this JCPOA. The IAEA will be requested to provide regular updates to the Board of Governors, and as provided for in this JCPOA, to the UN Security Council. All relevant rules and regulations of the IAEA with regard to the protection of information will be fully observed by all parties involved.

xi. All provisions and measures contained in this JCPOA are only for the purpose of its implementation between E3/EU+3 and Iran and should not be considered as setting precedents for any other state or for fundamental principles of international law and the rights and obligations under the NPT and other relevant instruments, as well as for internationally recognised principles and practices.

xii. Technical details of the implementation of this JCPOA are dealt with in the annexes to this document.

xiii. The EU and E3+3 countries and Iran, in the framework of the JCPOA, will cooperate, as appropriate, in the field of peaceful uses of nuclear energy and engage in mutually determined civil nuclear cooperation projects as detailed in Annex III, including through IAEA involvement.

xiv. The E3+3 will submit a draft resolution to the UN Security Council endorsing this JCPOA affirming that conclusion of this JCPOA marks a fundamental shift in its consideration of this issue and expressing its desire to build a new relationship with Iran. This UN Security Council resolution will also provide for the termination on Implementation Day of provisions imposed under previous resolutions; establishment of specific restrictions; and conclusion of consideration of the Iran nuclear issue by the UN Security Council 10 years after the Adoption Day.

xv. The provisions stipulated in this JCPOA will be implemented for their respective durations as set forth below and detailed in the annexes.

xvi. The E3/EU+3 and Iran will meet at the ministerial level every 2 years, or earlier if needed, in order to review and assess progress and to adopt appropriate decisions by consensus. Iran and E3/EU+3 will take the following voluntary measures within the timeframe as detailed in this JCPOA and its Annexes:

Nuclear

A. Enrichment, enrichment R&D, stockpiles

1. Iran's long term plan includes certain agreed limitations on all uranium enrichment and uranium enrichment-related activities including certain limitations on specific research and development (R&D) activities for the first 8 years, to be followed by gradual evolution, at a reasonable pace, to the next stage of its enrichment activities for exclusively peaceful purposes, as described in Annex I. Iran will abide by its voluntary commitments, as expressed in its own long-term enrichment and enrichment R&D plan to be submitted as part of the initial declaration for the Additional Protocol to Iran's Safeguards Agreement.

2. Iran will begin phasing out its IR-1 centrifuges in 10 years. During this period, Iran will keep its enrichment capacity at Natanz at up to a total installed uranium enrichment capacity of 5060 IR-1 centrifuges. Excess centrifuges and enrichment related infrastructure at Natanz will be stored under IAEA continuous monitoring, as specified in Annex I.

3. Iran will continue to conduct enrichment R&D in a manner that does not accumulate enriched uranium. Iran's enrichment R&D with uranium for 10 years will only include IR-4, IR-5, IR-6 and IR-8

centrifuges as laid out in Annex I, and Iran will not engage in other isotope separation technologies for enrichment of uranium as specified in Annex I. Iran will continue testing IR-6 and IR-8 centrifuges, and will commence testing of up to 30 IR-6 and IR-8 centrifuges after eight and a half years, as detailed in Annex I.

4. As Iran will be phasing out its IR-1 centrifuges, it will not manufacture or assemble other centrifuges, except as provided for in Annex I, and will replace failed centrifuges with centrifuges of the same type. Iran will manufacture advanced centrifuge machines only for the purposes specified in this JCPOA. From the end of the eighth year, and as described in Annex I, Iran will start to manufacture agreed numbers of IR-6 and IR-8 centrifuge machines without rotors and will store all of the manufactured machines at Natanz, under IAEA continuous monitoring until they are needed under Iran's long-term enrichment and enrichment R&D plan.

5. Based on its own long-term plan, for 15 years, Iran will carry out its uranium enrichment-related activities, including safeguarded R&D exclusively in the Natanz Enrichment facility, keep its level of uranium enrichment at up to 3.67%, and, at Fordow, refrain from any uranium enrichment and uranium enrichment R&D and from keeping any nuclear material.

6. Iran will convert the Fordow facility into a nuclear, physics and technology centre. International collaboration including in the form of scientific joint partnerships will be established in agreed areas of research. 1044 IR-1 centrifuges in six cascades will remain in one wing at Fordow. Two of these cascades will spin without uranium and will be transitioned, including through appropriate infrastructure modification, for stable isotope production.
The other four cascades with all associated infrastructure will remain idle. All other centrifuges and enrichment-related infrastructure will be removed and stored under IAEA continuous

monitoring as specified in Annex I.

7. During the 15 year period and as Iran gradually moves to meet international qualification standards for nuclear fuel produced in Iran, it will keep its uranium stockpile under 300 kg of up to 3.67% enriched uranium hexafluoride (UF6) or the equivalent in other chemical forms. The excess quantities are to be sold based on international prices and delivered to the international buyer in return for natural uranium delivered to Iran, or are to be down-blended to natural uranium level. Enriched uranium in fabricated fuel assemblies from Russia or other sources for use in Iran's nuclear reactors will not be counted against the above stated 300 kg UF6 stockpile, if the criteria set out in Annex I are met with regard to other sources. The Joint Commission will support assistance to Iran, including through IAEA technical cooperation as appropriate, in meeting international qualification standards for nuclear fuel produced in Iran. All remaining uranium oxide enriched to between 5% and 20% will be fabricated into fuel for the Tehran Research Reactor (TRR). Any additional fuel needed for the TRR will be made available to Iran at international market prices.

B. Arak, heavy water, reprocessing

8. Iran will redesign and rebuild a modernised heavy water research reactor in Arak, based on an agreed conceptual design, using fuel enriched up to 3.67 %, in a form of an international partnership which will certify the final design. The reactor will support peaceful nuclear research and radioisotope production for medical and industrial purposes. The redesigned and rebuilt Arak reactor will not produce weapons grade plutonium. Except for the first core load, all of the activities for redesigning and manufacturing of the fuel assemblies for the redesigned reactor will be carried out in Iran. All spent fuel from Arak will be shipped out of Iran for the lifetime of the reactor. This international partnership will include participating

E3/EU+3 parties, Iran and such other countries as may be mutually determined. Iran will take the leadership role as the owner and as the project manager and the E3/EU+3 and Iran will, before Implementation Day, conclude an official document which would define the responsibilities assumed by the E3/EU+3 participants.

9. Iran plans to keep pace with the trend of international technological advancement in relying on light water for its future power and research reactors with enhanced international cooperation, including assurance of supply of necessary fuel.

10. There will be no additional heavy water reactors or accumulation of heavy water in Iran for 15 years. All excess heavy water will be made available for export to the international market.

11. Iran intends to ship out all spent fuel for all future and present power and research nuclear reactors, for further treatment or disposition as provided for in relevant contracts to be duly concluded with the recipient party.

12. For 15 years Iran will not, and does not intend to thereafter, engage in any spent fuel reprocessing or construction of a facility capable of spent fuel reprocessing, or reprocessing R&D activities leading to a spent fuel reprocessing capability, with the sole exception of separation activities aimed exclusively at the production of medical and industrial radio-isotopes from irradiated enriched uranium targets.

C. Transparency and confidence building measures

13. Consistent with the respective roles of the President and Majlis (Parliament), Iran will provisionally apply the Additional Protocol to its Comprehensive Safeguards Agreement in accordance with Article

17(b) of the Additional Protocol, proceed with its ratification within the timeframe as detailed in Annex V and fully implement the modified Code 3.1 of the Subsidiary Arrangements to its Safeguards Agreement.

14. Iran will fully implement the "Roadmap for Clarification of Past and Present Outstanding Issues" agreed with the IAEA, containing arrangements to address past and present issues of concern relating to its nuclear programme as raised in the annex to the IAEA report of 8 November 2011 (GOV/2011/65). Full implementation of activities undertaken under the Roadmap by Iran will be completed by 15 October 2015, and subsequently the Director General will provide by 15 December 2015 the final assessment on the resolution of all past and present outstanding issues to the Board of Governors, and the E3+3, in their capacity as members of the Board of Governors, will submit a resolution to the Board of Governors for taking necessary actions, with a view to closing the issue, without prejudice to the competence of the Board of Governors.

15. Iran will allow the IAEA to monitor the implementation of the voluntary measures for their respective durations, as well as to implement transparency measures, as set out in this JCPOA and its Annexes. These measures include: a long-term IAEA presence in Iran; IAEA monitoring of uranium ore concentrate produced by Iran from all uranium ore concentrate plants for 25 years; containment and surveillance of centrifuge rotors and bellows for 20 years; use of IAEA approved and certified modern technologies including on-line enrichment measurement and electronic seals; and a reliable mechanism to ensure speedy resolution of IAEA access concerns for 15 years, as defined in Annex I.

16. Iran will not engage in activities, including at the R&D level that could contribute to the development of a nuclear explosive device, including uranium or plutonium metallurgy activities, as specified in

Annex I.

17. Iran will cooperate and act in accordance with the procurement channel in this JCPOA, as detailed in Annex IV, endorsed by the UN Security Council resolution.

Sanctions

18. The UN Security Council resolution endorsing this JCPOA will terminate all provisions of previous UN Security Council resolutions on the Iranian nuclear issue - 1696 (2006), 1737 (2006), 1747 (2007), 1803 (2008), 1835 (2008), 1929 (2010) and 2224 (2015) – simultaneously with the IAEA-verified implementation of agreed nuclear-related measures by Iran and will establish specific restrictions, as specified in Annex V.1

19. The EU will terminate all provisions of the EU Regulation, as subsequently amended, implementing all nuclear-related economic and financial sanctions, including related designations, simultaneously with the IAEA-verified implementation of agreed nuclear-related measures by Iran as specified in Annex V, which cover all sanctions and restrictive measures in the following areas as described in Annex II:

i. Transfers of funds between EU persons and entities, including financial institutions, and Iranian persons and entities, including financial institutions;
ii. Banking activities, including the establishment of new correspondent banking relationships and the opening of new branches and subsidiaries of Iranian banks in the territories of EU Member States;
iii. Provision of insurance and reinsurance;

iv. Supply of specialised financial messaging services, including SWIFT, for persons and entities set out in Attachment 1 to Annex II, including the Central Bank of Iran and Iranian financial institutions;

v. Financial support for trade with Iran (export credit, guarantees or insurance);

vi. Commitments for grants, financial assistance and concessional loans to the Government of Iran;

vii. Transactions in public or public-guaranteed bonds;

viii. Import and transport of Iranian oil, petroleum products, gas and petrochemical products;

ix. Export of key equipment or technology for the oil, gas and petrochemical sectors;

x. Investment in the oil, gas and petrochemical sectors;

xi. Export of key naval equipment and technology;

xii. Design and construction of cargo vessels and oil tankers;

xiii. Provision of flagging and classification services;

xiv. Access to EU airports of Iranian cargo flights;

xv. Export of gold, precious metals and diamonds;

xvi. Delivery of Iranian banknotes and coinage;

xvii. Export of graphite, raw or semi-finished metals such as aluminum and steel, and export or software for integrating industrial processes;

xviii. Designation of persons, entities and bodies (asset freeze and visa ban) set out in Attachment 1 to Annex II; and

xix. Associated services for each of the categories above.

20. The EU will terminate all provisions of the EU Regulation implementing all EU proliferation-related sanctions, including related designations, 8 years after Adoption Day or when the IAEA has reached the Broader Conclusion that all nuclear material in Iran remains in peaceful activities, whichever is earlier.

21. The United States will cease the application, and will continue to do so, in accordance with this JCPOA of the sanctions specified in Annex II to take effect simultaneously with the IAEA-verified

implementation of the agreed nuclear related measures by Iran as specified in Annex V. Such sanctions cover the following areas as described in Annex II:

i. Financial and banking transactions with Iranian banks and financial institutions as specified in Annex II, including the Central Bank of Iran and specified individuals and entities identified as Government of Iran by the Office of Foreign Assets Control on the Specially Designated Nationals and Blocked Persons List (SDN List), as set out in Attachment 3 to Annex II (including the opening and maintenance of correspondent and payable through-accounts at non-U.S. financial institutions, investments, foreign exchange transactions and letters of credit);

ii. Transactions in Iranian Rial;

iii. Provision of U.S. banknotes to the Government of Iran;

iv. Bilateral trade limitations on Iranian revenues abroad, including limitations on their transfer;

v. Purchase, subscription to, or facilitation of the issuance of Iranian sovereign debt, including governmental bonds;

vi. Financial messaging services to the Central Bank of Iran and Iranian financial institutions set out in Attachment 3 to Annex II;

vii. Underwriting services, insurance, or reinsurance;

viii. Efforts to reduce Iran's crude oil sales;

ix. Investment, including participation in joint ventures, goods, services, information, technology and technical expertise and support for Iran's oil, gas and petrochemical sectors;

x. Purchase, acquisition, sale, transportation or marketing of petroleum, petrochemical products and natural gas from Iran;

xi. Export, sale or provision of refined petroleum products and petrochemical products to Iran;

xii. Transactions with Iran's energy sector;

xiii. Transactions with Iran's shipping and shipbuilding sectors and port operators;

xiv. Trade in gold and other precious metals;

xv. Trade with Iran in graphite, raw or semi-finished metals such as aluminum and steel, coal, and software for integrating industrial processes;

xvi. Sale, supply or transfer of goods and services used in connection with Iran's automotive sector;

xvii. Sanctions on associated services for each of the categories above;

xviii. Remove individuals and entities set out in Attachment 3 to Annex II from the SDN List, the Foreign Sanctions Evaders List, and/or the Non-SDN Iran Sanctions Act List; and

xix. Terminate Executive Orders 13574, 13590, 13622, and 13645, and Sections5 – 7 and 15 of Executive Order 13628.

22. The United States will, as specified in Annex II and in accordance with Annex V, allow for the sale of commercial passenger aircraft and related parts and services to Iran; license non-U.S. persons that are owned or controlled by a U.S. person to engage in activities with Iran consistent with this JCPOA; and license the importation into the United States of Iranian-origin carpets and foodstuffs.

23. Eight years after Adoption Day or when the IAEA has reached the Broader Conclusion that all nuclear material in Iran remains in peaceful activities, whichever is earlier, the United States will seek such legislative action as may be appropriate to terminate, or modify to effectuate the termination of, the sanctions specified in Annex II on the acquisition of nuclear-related commodities and services for nuclear activities contemplated in this JCPOA, to be consistent with the U.S. approach to other non-nuclear-weapon states under the NPT.

24. The E3/EU and the United States specify in Annex II a full and complete list of all nuclear-related sanctions or restrictive measures and will lift them in accordance with Annex V. Annex II also

specifies the effects of the lifting of sanctions beginning on "Implementation Day". If at any time following the Implementation Day, Iran believes that any other nuclear-related sanction or restrictive measure of the E3/EU+3 is preventing the full implementation of the sanctions lifting as specified in this JCPOA, the JCPOA participant in question will consult with Iran with a view to resolving the issue and, if they concur that lifting of this sanction or restrictive measure is appropriate, the JCPOA participant in question will take appropriate action. If they are not able to resolve the issue, Iran or any member of the E3/EU+3 may refer the issue to the Joint Commission.

25. If a law at the state or local level in the United States is preventing the implementation of the sanctions lifting as specified in this JCPOA, the United States will take appropriate steps, taking into account all available authorities, with a view to achieving such implementation. The United States will actively encourage officials at the state or local level to take into account the changes in the U.S. policy reflected in the lifting of sanctions under this JCPOA and to refrain from actions inconsistent with this change in policy.

26. The EU will refrain from re-introducing or re-imposing the sanctions that it has terminated implementing under this JCPOA, without prejudice to the dispute resolution process provided for under this JCPOA. There will be no new nuclear related UN Security Council sanctions and no new EU nuclear-related sanctions or restrictive measures. The United States will make best efforts in good faith to sustain this JCPOA and to prevent interference with the realisation of the full benefit by Iran of the sanctions lifting specified in Annex II. The U.S. Administration, acting consistent with the respective roles of the President and the Congress, will refrain from re-introducing or re-imposing the sanctions specified in Annex II that it has ceased applying under this JCPOA, without prejudice to the dispute resolution process provided for under this JCPOA. The

U.S. Administration, acting consistent with the respective roles of the President and the Congress, will refrain from imposing new nuclear-related sanctions. Iran has stated that it will treat such a re-introduction or re-imposition of the sanctions specified in Annex II, or such an imposition of new nuclear-related sanctions, as grounds to cease performing its commitments under this JCPOA in whole or in part.

27. The E3/EU+3 will take adequate administrative and regulatory measures to ensure clarity and effectiveness with respect to the lifting of sanctions under this JCPOA. The EU and its Member States as well as the United States will issue relevant guidelines and make publicly accessible statements on the details of sanctions or restrictive measures which have been lifted under this JCPOA. The EU and its Member States and the United States commit to consult with Iran regarding the content of such guidelines and statements, on a regular basis and whenever appropriate.

28. The E3/EU+3 and Iran commit to implement this JCPOA in good faith and in a constructive atmosphere, based on mutual respect, and to refrain from any action inconsistent with the letter, spirit and intent of this JCPOA that would undermine its successful implementation. Senior Government officials of the E3/EU+3 and M Iran will make every effort to support the successful implementation of this JCPOA including in their public statements2. The E3/EU+3 will take all measures required to lift sanctions and will refrain from imposing exceptional discriminatory regulatory and procedural requirements in lieu of the sanctions and restrictive measures covered by the JCPOA.

29. The EU and its Member States and the United States, consistent with their respective laws, will refrain from any policy specifically intended to directly and adversely affect the normalisation of trade and economic relations with Iran inconsistent with their

commitments not to undermine the successful implementation of this JCPOA.

30. The E3/EU+3 will not apply sanctions or restrictive measures to persons or entities for engaging in activities covered by the lifting of sanctions provided for in this JCPOA, provided that such activities are otherwise consistent with E3/EU+3 laws and regulations in effect. Following the lifting of sanctions under this JCPOA as specified in Annex II, ongoing investigations on possible infringements of such sanctions may be reviewed in accordance with applicable national laws.

31. Consistent with the timing specified in Annex V, the EU and its Member States will terminate the implementation of the measures applicable to designated entities and individuals, including the Central Bank of Iran and other Iranian banks and financial institutions, as detailed in Annex II and the attachments thereto.
2 'Government officials' for the U.S. means senior officials of the U.S. Administration. 15 Consistent with the timing specified in Annex V, the United States will remove designation of certain entities and individuals on the Specially Designated Nationals and Blocked Persons List, and entities and individuals listed on the Foreign Sanctions Evaders List, as detailed in Annex II and the attachments thereto.

32. EU and E3+3 countries and international participants will engage in joint projects with Iran, including through IAEA technical cooperation projects, in the field of peaceful nuclear technology, including nuclear power plants, research reactors, fuel fabrication, agreed joint advanced R&D such as fusion, establishment of a state-of the- art regional nuclear medical centre, personnel training, nuclear safety and security, and environmental protection, as detailed in Annex III. They will take necessary measures, as appropriate, for the implementation of these projects.

33. The E3/EU+3 and Iran will agree on steps to ensure Iran's access in areas of trade, technology, finance and energy. The EU will further explore possible areas for cooperation between the EU, its Member States and Iran, and in this context consider the use of available instruments such as export credits to facilitate trade, project financing and investment in Iran.

Implementation Plan

34. Iran and the E3/EU+3 will implement their JCPOA commitments according to the sequence specified in Annex V. The milestones for implementation are as follows:

i. Finalisation Day is the date on which negotiations of this JCPOA are concluded among the E3/EU+3 and Iran, to be followed promptly by submission of the resolution endorsing this JCPOA to the UN Security Council for adoption without delay.

ii. Adoption Day is the date 90 days after the endorsement of this JCPOA by the UN Security Council, or such earlier date as may be determined by mutual consent of the JCPOA participants, at which time this JCPOA and the commitments in this JCPOA come into effect. Beginning on that date, JCPOA participants will make necessary arrangements and preparations for the implementation of their JCPOA commitments.

iii. Implementation Day is the date on which, simultaneously with the IAEA report verifying implementation by Iran of the nuclear-related measures described in Sections 15.1 and 15.11 of Annex V, the EU and the United States take the actions described in Sections 16 and 17 of Annex V respectively and in accordance with the UN

Security Council resolution, the actions described in Section 18 of Annex V occur at the UN level.

iv. Transition Day is the date 8 years after Adoption Day or the date on which the Director General of the IAEA submits a report stating that the IAEA has reached the Broader Conclusion that all nuclear material in Iran remains in peaceful activities, whichever is earlier. On that date, the EU and the United States will take the actions described in Sections 20 and 21 of Annex V respectively and Iran will seek, consistent with the Constitutional roles of the President and Parliament, ratification of the Additional Protocol.

v. UN Security Council resolution Termination Day is the date on which the UN Security Council resolution endorsing this JCPOA terminates according to its terms, which is to be 10 years from

Adoption Day provided that the provisions of previous resolutions have not been reinstated. On that date, the EU will take the actions described in Section 25 of Annex V.

35. The sequence and milestones set forth above and in Annex V are without prejudice to the duration of JCPOA commitments stated in this JCPOA.

Dispute Resolution Mechanism

36. If Iran believed that any or all of the E3/EU+3 were not meeting their commitments under this JCPOA, Iran could refer the issue to the Joint Commission for resolution; similarly, if any of the E3/EU+3 believed that Iran was not meeting its commitments under this JCPOA, any of the E3/EU+3 could do the same. The Joint Commission would have 15 days to resolve the issue, unless the time period was extended by consensus. After Joint Commission consideration, any participant could refer the issue to Ministers of Foreign Affairs, if it believed the compliance issue had not been resolved. Ministers would have 15 days to resolve the issue, unless the time period was extended by consensus. After Joint Commission consideration – in parallel with (or in lieu of) review at the Ministerial level - either the complaining participant or the participant whose performance is in question could request that the issue be considered by an Advisory Board, which would consist of three members (one each appointed by the participants in the dispute and a third independent member). The Advisory Board should provide a non-binding opinion on the compliance issue within 15 days.

If, after this 30-day process the issue is not resolved, the Joint Commission would consider the opinion of the Advisory Board for no more than 5 days in order to resolve the issue. If the issue still has not been resolved to the satisfaction of the complaining participant, and if the complaining participant deems the issue to constitute significant non-performance, then that participant could treat the unresolved issue as grounds to cease performing its commitments under this JCPOA in whole or in part and/or notify the UN Security Council that it believes the issue constitutes significant non-performance.

37. Upon receipt of the notification from the complaining participant, as described above, including a description of the good-faith efforts the participant made to exhaust the dispute resolution process specified in this JCPOA, the UN Security Council, in accordance with its procedures, shall vote on a resolution to continue the sanctions lifting. If the resolution described above has not been adopted within 30 days of the notification, then the provisions of the old UN Security Council resolutions would be re-imposed, unless the UN Security Council decides otherwise. In such event, these provisions would not apply with retroactive effect to contracts signed between any party and Iran or Iranian individuals and entities prior to the date of application, provided that the activities contemplated under and execution of such contracts are consistent with this JCPOA and the previous and current UN Security Council resolutions. The UN Security Council, expressing its intention to prevent the reapplication of the provisions if the issue giving rise to the notification is resolved within this period, intends to take into account the views of the States involved in the issue and any opinion on the issue of the Advisory Board. Iran has stated that if sanctions are reinstated in whole or in part, Iran will treat that as grounds to cease performing its commitments under this JCPOA in whole or in part.

CHAPTER THREE

Content of Annex I

Nuclear-Related Measures

A. General

1. The sequence of implementation of the commitments detailed in this Annex is specified in Annex V to the Joint Comprehensive Plan of Action (JCPOA). Unless otherwise specified, the durations of the commitments in this Annex are from Implementation Day.

B. Arak heavy water research reactor

2. Iran will modernise the Arak heavy water research reactor to support peaceful nuclear research and radioisotopes production for medical and industrial purposes. Iran will redesign and rebuild the reactor, based on the agreed conceptual design (as attached to this Annex) to support its peaceful nuclear research and production needs and purposes, including testing of fuel pins and assembly prototypes and structural materials. The design will be such as minimise the production of plutonium and not to produce weapon-grade plutonium in normal operation. The power of the redesigned reactor will not exceed 20 MWth. The E3/EU+3 and Iran share the understanding that the parameters in the conceptual design are subject to possible and necessary adjustments in developing the final design while fully preserving the abovementioned purposes and principles of modernisation.

3. Iran will not pursue construction at the existing unfinished reactor based on its original design and will remove the existing calandria and retain it in Iran. The calandria will be made inoperable by filling any openings in the calandria with concrete such that the IAEA can verify that it will not be usable for a future nuclear application. In redesigning and reconstructing of the modernized Arak heavy water research reactor, Iran will maximise the use of existing infrastructure already installed at the current Arak research reactor.

4. Iran will take the leadership role as the owner and as the project manager, and have responsibility for overall implementation of the Arak modernisation project, with E3/EU+3 participants assuming responsibilities regarding the modernisation of the Arak reactor as described in this Annex. A Working Group composed of E3/EU+3 participants will be established to facilitate the redesigning and rebuilding of the reactor. An international partnership composed of Iran and the Working Group would implement the Arak modernisation project. The Working Group could be enlarged to include other countries by consensus of the participants of the Working Group and Iran. E3/EU+3 participants and Iran will conclude an official document expressing their strong commitments to the Arak modernisation project in advance of Implementation Day which would provide an assured path forward to modernize the reactor and would define the responsibilities assumed by the E3/EU+3 participants, and subsequently contracts would be concluded. The participants of the Working Group will provide assistance needed by Iran for redesigning and rebuilding the reactor, consistent with their respective national laws, in such a manner as to enable the safe and timely construction and commissioning of the modernised reactor.

5. Iran and the Working Group will cooperate to develop the final design of the modernised reactor and the design of the subsidiary laboratories to be carried out by Iran, and review conformity with

international safety standards, such that the reactor can be licensed by the relevant Iranian regulatory authority for commissioning and operation. The final design of the modernised reactor and the design of the subsidiary laboratories will be submitted to the Joint Commission. The Joint Commission will aim to complete its review and endorsement within three months after the submission of the final design. If the Joint Commission does not complete its review and endorsement within three months, Iran could raise the issue through the dispute resolution mechanism envisaged by this JCPOA.

6. The IAEA will monitor the construction and report to the Working Group for confirmation that the construction of the modernised reactor is consistent with the approved final design.

7. As the project manager, Iran will take responsibility for the construction efforts. E3/EU+3 parties will, consistent with their national laws, take appropriate administrative, legal, technical, and regulatory measures to support co-operation. E3/EU+3 parties will support the purchase by Iran, the transfer and supply of necessary materials, equipment, instrumentation and control systems and technologies required for the construction of the redesigned reactor, through the mechanism established by this JCPOA, as well as through exploration of relevant funding contributions.

8. E3/EU+3 parties will also support and facilitate the timely and safe construction of the modernized Arak reactor and its subsidiary laboratories, upon request by Iran, through IAEA technical cooperation if appropriate, including but not limited to technical and financial assistance, supply of required materials and equipment, state-of-the-art instrumentation and control systems and equipment and support for licensing and authorization.

9. The redesigned reactor will use up to 3.67 percent enriched uranium in the form of UO2 with a mass of approximately 350 kg of

UO2 in a full core load, with a fuel design to be reviewed and approved by the Joint Commission. The international partnership with the participation of Iran will fabricate the initial fuel core load for the reactor outside Iran. The international partnership will cooperate with Iran, including through technical assistance, to fabricate, test and license fuel fabrication capabilities in Iran for subsequent fuel core reloads for future use with this reactor. Destructive and non-destructive testing of this fuel including Post-Irradiation-Examination (PIE) will take place in one of the participating countries outside of Iran and that country will work with Iran to license the subsequent fuel fabricated in Iran for the use in the redesigned reactor under IAEA monitoring.

10. Iran will not produce or test natural uranium pellets, fuel pins or fuel assemblies, which are specifically designed for the support of the originally designed Arak reactor, designated by the IAEA. Iran will store under IAEA continuous monitoring all existing natural uranium pellets and IR-40 fuel assemblies until the modernised Arak reactor becomes operational, at which point these natural uranium pellets and IR-40 fuel assemblies will be converted to UNH, or exchanged with an equivalent quantity of natural uranium. Iran will make the necessary technical modifications to the natural uranium fuel production process line that was intended to supply fuel for the IR-40 reactor design; such that it can be used for the fabrication of the fuel reloads for the modernised Arak reactor.

11. All spent fuel from the redesigned Arak reactor, regardless of its origin, for the lifetime of the reactor, will be shipped out of Iran to a mutually determined location in E3/EU+3 countries or third countries, for further treatment or disposition as provided for in relevant contracts to be concluded, consistent with national laws, with the recipient party, within one year from the unloading from the reactor or whenever deemed to be safe for transfer by the recipient country.

12. Iran will submit the DIQ of the redesigned reactor to the IAEA which will include information on the planned radio-isotope production and reactor operation programme. The reactor will be operated under IAEA monitoring.

13. Iran will operate the Fuel Manufacturing Plant only to produce fuel assemblies for light water reactors and reloads for the modernized Arak reactor.

C. Heavy water production plant

14. All excess heavy water which is beyond Iran's needs for the modernised Arak research reactor, the Zero power heavy water reactor, quantities needed for medical research and production of deuterate solutions and chemical compounds including, where appropriate, contingency stocks, will be made available for export to the international market based on international prices and delivered to the international buyer for 15 years. Iran's needs, consistent with the parameters above, are estimated to be 130 metric tonnes of nuclear grade heavy water or its equivalent in different enrichments prior to commissioning of the modernised Arak research reactor, and 90 metric tonnes after the commissioning, including the amount contained in the reactor.

15. Iran will inform the IAEA about the inventory and the production of the HWPP and will allow the IAEA to monitor the quantities of the heavy water stocks and the amount of heavy water produced, including through IAEA visits, as requested, to the HWPP.

D. Other reactors

16. Consistent with its plan, Iran will keep pace with the trend of international technological advancement in relying only on light

water for its future nuclear power and research reactors with enhanced international cooperation including assurances of supply of necessary fuel.

17. Iran intends to ship out all spent fuel for all future and present nuclear power and research reactors, for further treatment or disposition as provided for in relevant contracts to be concluded consistent with national laws with the recipient party.

E. **Spent fuel reprocessing activities**

18. For 15 years Iran will not, and does not intend to thereafter, engage in any spent fuel reprocessing or spent fuel reprocessing R&D activities. For the purpose of this annex, spent fuel includes all types of irradiated fuel.

19. For 15 years Iran will not, and does not intend to thereafter, reprocess spent fuel except for irradiated enriched uranium targets for production of radio-isotopes for medical and peaceful industrial purposes.

20. For 15 years Iran will not, and does not intend to thereafter, develop, acquire or build facilities capable of separation of plutonium, uranium or neptunium from spent fuel or from fertile targets, other than for production of radio-isotopes for medical and peaceful industrial purposes.

21. For 15 years, Iran will only develop, acquire, build, or operate hot cells (containing a cell or interconnected cells), shielded cells or shielded glove boxes with dimensions less than 6 cubic meters in volume compatible with the specifications set out in Annex I of the Additional Protocol. These will be collocated with the modernised Arak research reactor, the Tehran Research Reactor, and radio-medicine production complexes, and only capable of the separation

and processing of industrial or medical isotopes and non-destructive PIE. For 15 years, Iran will develop, acquire, build, or operate hot cells (containing a cell or interconnected cells), shielded cells or shielded glove boxes with dimensions beyond 6 cubic meters in volume and specifications set out in Annex I of the Additional Protocol, only after approval by the Joint Commission.

22. The E3/EU+3 are ready to facilitate all of the destructive and non-destructive examinations on fuel elements and/or fuel assembly prototypes including PIE for all fuel fabricated in or outside Iran and irradiated in Iran, using their existing facilities outside Iran. Except for the Arak research reactor complex, Iran will not develop, build, acquire or operate hot cells capable of performing PIE or seek to acquire equipment to build/develop such a capability, for 15 years.

23. For 15 years, in addition to continuing current fuel testing activities at the TRR, Iran will undertake non-destructive post irradiation examination (PIE) of fuel pins, fuel assembly prototypes and structural materials. These examinations will be exclusively at the Arak research reactor complex. However, the E3/EU+3 will make available their facilities to conduct destructive testing with Iranian specialists, as agreed. The hot cells at the Arak research reactor in which nondestructive PIE are performed will not be physically interconnected to cells that process or handle materials for the production of medical or industrial radioisotopes.

24. For 15 years, Iran will not engage in producing or acquiring plutonium or uranium metals or their alloys, or conducting R&D on plutonium or uranium (or their alloys) metallurgy, or casting, forming, or machining plutonium or uranium metal.

25. Iran will not produce, seek, or acquire separated plutonium, highly enriched uranium (defined as 20% or greater uranium-235), or uranium-233, or neptunium-237 (except for use as laboratory

standards or in instruments using neptunium-237) for 15 years.

26. If Iran seeks to initiate R&D on uranium metal based TRR fuel in small agreed quantities after 10 years and before 15 years, Iran will present its plan to, and seek approval by, the Joint Commission.

F. **Enrichment capacity**
27. Iran will keep its enrichment capacity at no more than 5060 IR-1 centrifuge machines in no more than 30 cascades in their current configurations in currently operating units at the Natanz Fuel Enrichment Plant (FEP) for 10 years.

28. Iran will keep its level of uranium enrichment at up to 3.67 percent for 15 years.

29. Iran will remove the following excess centrifuges and infrastructure not associated with 5060 IR-1 centrifuges in FEP, which will be stored at Natanz in Hall B of FEP under IAEA continuous monitoring:

29.1. All excess centrifuge machines, including IR-2m centrifuges. Excess IR-1 centrifuges will be used for the replacement of failed or damaged centrifuges of the same type on a one-for-one basis.

29.2. UF6 pipe-work including sub headers, valves and pressure transducers at cascade level, and frequency inverters, and UF6 withdrawal equipment from one of the withdrawal stations, which is currently not in service, including its vacuum pumps and chemical traps.

30. For the purpose of this Annex, the IAEA will confirm through the established practice the failed or damaged status of centrifuge machines before removal.

31. For 15 years, Iran will install gas centrifuge machines, or enrichment-related infrastructure, whether suitable for uranium enrichment, research and development, or stable isotope enrichment, exclusively at the locations and for the activities specified under this JCPOA.

G. Centrifuges research and development

32. Iran will continue to conduct enrichment R&D in a manner that does not accumulate enriched uranium. For 10 years and consistent with its enrichment R&D plan, Iran's enrichment R&D with uranium will only include IR-4, IR-5, IR-6 and IR-8 centrifuges. Mechanical testing on up to two single centrifuges for each type will be carried out only on the IR-2m, IR-4, IR-5, IR-6, IR-6s, IR-7 and IR-8. Iran will build or test, with or without uranium, only those gas centrifuges specified in this JCPOA.

33. Consistent with its plan, Iran will continue working with the 164-machine IR-2m cascade at PFEP in order to complete the necessary tests until 30 November 2015 or the day of implementation of this JCPOA, whichever comes later, and after that it will take these machines out of the PFEP and store them under IAEA continuous monitoring at Natanz in Hall B of FEP.

34. Consistent with its plan, Iran will continue working with the 164-machine IR-4 cascade at PFEP in order to complete the necessary tests until 30 November 2015 or the day of implementation of this JCPOA, whichever comes later, and after that it will take these machines out of the PFEP and store them under IAEA continuous monitoring at Natanz in Hall B of FEP.

35. Iran will continue the testing of a single IR-4 centrifuge machine and IR-4 centrifuge cascade of up to 10 centrifuge machines for 10

years.

36. Iran will test a single IR-5 centrifuge machine for 10 years.

37. Iran will continue testing of the IR-6 on single centrifuge machines and its intermediate cascades and will commence testing of up to 30 centrifuge machines from one and a half years before the end of year 10. Iran will proceed from single centrifuge machines and small cascades to intermediate cascades in a logical sequence.

38. Iran will commence, upon start of implementation of the JCPOA, testing of the IR- 8 on single centrifuge machines and its intermediate cascades and will commence the testing of up to 30 centrifuges machines from one and a half years before the end of year 10. Iran will proceed from single centrifuges to small cascades to intermediate cascades in a logical sequence.

39. For 10 years, Iran, consistent with the established practice, will recombine the enriched and depleted streams from the IR-6 and IR-8 cascades through the use of welded pipe-work on withdrawal main headers in a manner that precludes the withdrawal of enriched and depleted uranium materials and verified by the IAEA.

40. For 15 years, Iran will conduct all testing of centrifuges with uranium only at the PFEP. Iran will conduct all mechanical testing of centrifuges only at the PFEP and the Tehran Research Centre.

41. For the purpose of adapting PFEP to the R&D activities in the enrichment and enrichment R&D plan, Iran will remove all centrifuges except those needed for testing as described in the relevant paragraphs above, except for the IR-1 cascade (No. 1) as described below. For the full IR-1 cascade (No. 6), Iran will modify associated infrastructure by removing UF6 pipe-work, including sub-headers, valves and pressure transducers at cascade level, and

frequency inverters. The IR-1 cascade (No. 1) centrifuges will be kept but made inoperable, as verified by the IAEA, through the removal of centrifuge rotors and the injection of epoxy resin into the sub headers, feeding, product, and tails pipe-work, and the removal of controls and electrical systems for vacuum, power and cooling. Excess centrifuges and infrastructure will be stored at Natanz in Hall B of FEP under IAEA continuous monitoring. The R&D space in line No. 6 will be left empty until Iran needs to use it for its R&D programme.

42. Consistent with the activities in the enrichment and enrichment R&D plan, Iran will maintain the cascade infrastructure for testing of single centrifuges and small and intermediate cascades in two R&D lines (No. 2 and No. 3) and will adapt two other lines (No. 4 and No. 5) with infrastructure similar to that for lines No. 2 and No. 3 in order to enable future R&D activities as specified in this JCPOA. Adaptation will include modification of all UF6 pipe-work (including removal of all sub headers except as agreed as needed for the R&D programme) and associated instrumentation to be compatible with single centrifuges and small and intermediate cascade testing instead of full scale testing.

43. Consistent with its plan and internationally established practices, Iran intends to continue R&D on new types of centrifuges through computer modelling and simulations, including at universities. For any such project to proceed to a prototype stage for mechanical testing within 10 years, a full presentation to, and approval by, the Joint Commission is needed.

H. **Fordow fuel enrichment plant**

44. The Fordow Fuel Enrichment Plant (FFEP) will be converted into a nuclear, physics, and technology centre and international collaboration will be encouraged in agreed areas of research. The

Joint Commission will be informed in advance of the specific projects that will be undertaken at Fordow.

45. Iran will not conduct any uranium enrichment or any uranium enrichment related R&D and will have no nuclear material at the Fordow Fuel Enrichment Plant (FFEP) for 15 years.

46. For 15 years, Iran will maintain no more than 1044 IR-1 centrifuge machines at one wing of the FFEP of which:

46.1. Two cascades that have not experienced UF6 before will be modified for the production of stable isotopes. The transition to stable isotope production of these cascades at FFEP will be conducted in joint partnership between the Russian Federation and Iran on the basis of arrangements to be mutually agreed upon. To prepare these two cascades for installation of a new cascade architecture appropriate for stable isotope production by the joint partnership Iran will remove the connection to the UF6 feed main header, and move cascade UF6 pipework (except for the dump line in order to maintain vacuum) to storage in Fordow under IAEA continuous monitoring. The Joint Commission will be informed about the conceptual framework of stable isotope production at FFEP.

46.2. For four cascades with all associated infrastructure remaining except for pipe-work that enables crossover tandem connections, two will be placed in an idle state, not spinning. The other two cascades will continue to spin until the transition to stable isotope production described in the previous subparagraph has been completed. Upon completion of the transition to stable isotope production described in the previous subparagraph, these two spinning cascades will be placed in an idle state, not spinning.

47. Iran will:

47.1. Remove the other 2 cascades of IR-1 centrifuges from this wing, by removing all centrifuges and cascade UF6 pipe-work, including sub headers, valves and pressure transducers at cascade level, and frequency inverters.

47.2. Also subsequently remove cascade electrical cabling, individual cascade control cabinets and vacuum pumps. All these excess centrifuges and infrastructure will be stored at Natanz in Hall B of FEP under IAEA continuous monitoring.

48. Iran will:

48.1. remove all excess centrifuges and uranium enrichment related infrastructure from the other wing of the FFEP. This will include removal of all centrifuges and UF6 pipe-work, including sub headers, valves and pressure gauges and transducers, and frequency inverters and converters, and UF6 feed and withdrawal stations.

48.2. Also subsequently remove cascade electrical cabling, individual cascade control cabinets, vacuum pumps and centrifuge mounting blocks. All these excess centrifuges and infrastructure will be stored at Natanz in Hall B of FEP under IAEA continuous monitoring.

49. Centrifuges from the four idle cascades may be used for the replacement of failed or damaged centrifuges in stable isotope production at Fordow.

50. Iran will limit its stable isotope production activities with gas centrifuges to the
FFEP for 15 years and will use no more than 348 IR-1 centrifuges for these activities at the FFEP. The associated R&D activities in Iran will occur at the FFEP and at Iran's declared and monitored centrifuge manufacturing facilities for testing, modification and balancing these IR-1 centrifuges.

51. The IAEA will establish a baseline for the amount of uranium legacy from past enrichment operations that will remain in Fordow. Iran will permit the IAEA regular access, including daily as requested by the IAEA, access to the FFEP in order to monitor Iran's production of stable isotopes and the absence of undeclared nuclear material and activities at the FFEP for 15 years.

I. **Other aspects of enrichment**

52. Iran will abide by its voluntary commitments as expressed in its own long term enrichment and enrichment R&D plan to be submitted as part of the initial declaration described in Article 2 of the Additional Protocol.1 The IAEA will confirm on an annual basis, for the duration of the plan that the nature and scope and scale of Iran's enrichment and enrichment R&D activities are in line with this plan.

53. Iran will start to install necessary infrastructure for the IR-8 at Natanz in Hall B of FEP after year 10.

54. An agreed template for describing different centrifuge types (IR-1, IR-2m, IR-4, IR-5, IR-6, IR-6s, IR-7, and IR-8) and the associated definitions need to be accomplished by implementation day.

55. An agreed procedure for measuring IR-1, IR-2m and IR-4 centrifuge performance data needs to be accomplished by implementation day.

J. **Uranium stocks and fuels**
Iran will permit the IAEA to share the content of the enrichment and enrichment R&D plan, as submitted as part of the initial declaration, with the Joint Commission participants.

56. Iran will maintain a total enriched uranium stockpile of no more than 300 kg of up to 3.67% enriched uranium hexafluoride (or the equivalent in different chemical forms) for 15 years.

57. All enriched uranium hexafluoride in excess of 300 kg of up to 3.67% enriched UF6 (or the equivalent in different chemical forms) will be down blended to natural uranium level or be sold on the international market and delivered to the international buyer in return for natural uranium delivered to Iran. Iran will enter into a commercial contract with an entity outside Iran for the purchase and transfer of its enriched uranium stockpile in excess of 300 kg UF6 in return for natural uranium delivered to Iran. The E3/EU+3 will facilitate, where applicable, the conclusion and implementation of this contract. Iran may choose to seek to sell excess enriched uranium to the IAEA fuel bank in Kazakhstan when the fuel bank becomes operational.

58. All uranium oxide enriched to between 5% and 20% will be fabricated into fuel plates for the Tehran Research Reactor or transferred, based on a commercial transaction, outside of Iran or diluted to an enrichment level of 3.67% or less.
Scrap oxide and other forms not in plates that cannot be fabricated into TRR fuel plates will be transferred, based on a commercial transaction, outside of Iran or diluted to an enrichment level of 3.67% or less. In case of future supply of 19.75% enriched uranium oxide (U3O8) for TRR fuel plates fabrication, all scrap oxide and other forms not in plates that cannot be fabricated into TRR fuel plates, containing uranium enriched to between 5% and 20%, will be transferred, based on a commercial transaction, outside of Iran or diluted to an enrichment level of 3.67% or less within 6 months of its production. Scrap plates will be transferred based on a commercial transaction, outside Iran. The commercial transactions should be structured to return an equivalent amount of natural uranium to Iran.

For 15 years, Iran will not build or operate facilities for converting fuel plates or scrap back to UF6.

59. Russian designed, fabricated and licensed fuel assemblies for use in Russian supplied reactors in Iran do not count against the 300 kg UF6 stockpile limit. Enriched uranium in fabricated fuel assemblies from other sources outside of Iran for use in Iran's nuclear research and power reactors, including those which will be fabricated outside of Iran for the initial fuel load of the modernised Arak research reactor, which are certified by the fuel supplier and the appropriate Iranian authority to meet international standards, will not count against the 300 kg UF6 stockpile limit. The Joint Commission will establish a Technical Working Group with the goal of enabling fuel to be fabricated in Iran while adhering to the agreed stockpile parameters (300 kg of up to 3.67 % enriched UF6 or the equivalent in different chemical forms). This Technical Working Group will also, within one year, work to develop objective technical criteria for assessing whether fabricated fuel and its intermediate products can be readily converted to UF6. Enriched uranium in fabricated fuel assemblies and its intermediate products manufactured in Iran and certified to meet international standards, including those for the

modernised Arak research reactor will not count against the 300 kg UF6 stockpile limit provided the Technical Working Group of the Joint Commission approves that such fuel assemblies and their intermediate products cannot be readily reconverted into UF6. This could for instance be achieved through impurities (e.g. burnable poisons or otherwise) contained in fuels or through the fuel being in a chemical form such that direct conversion back to UF6 would be technically difficult without dissolution and purification. The objective technical criteria will guide the approval process of the Technical Working Group. The IAEA will monitor the fuel fabrication process for any fuel produced in Iran to verify that the fuel and intermediate products comport with the fuel fabrication process that was approved by the Technical Working Group. The Joint Commission will also support assistance to Iran including through IAEA technical cooperation as appropriate, in meeting international qualification standards for nuclear fuel produced by Iran.

60. Iran will seek to enter into a commercial contract with entities outside Iran for the purchase of fuel for the TRR and enriched uranium targets. The E3/EU+3 will facilitate, as needed, the conclusion and implementation of this contract. In the case of lack of conclusion of a contract with a fuel supplier, E3/EU+3 will supply a quantity of 19.75% enriched uranium oxide (U3O8) and deliver to Iran, exclusively for the purpose of fabrication in Iran of fuel for the TRR and enriched uranium targets for the lifetime of the reactor. This 19.75% enriched uranium oxide (U3O8) will be supplied in increments no greater than approximately 5 kg and each new increment will be provided only when the previous increment of this material has been verified by the IAEA to have been mixed with aluminum to make fuel for the TRR or fabricated into enriched uranium targets. Iran will notify the E3/EU+3 within 2 year before the contingency of TRR fuel will be exhausted in order to have the uranium oxide available 6 months before the end of the 2 year time.

K. Centrifuge manufacturing

61. Consistent with its enrichment and enrichment R&D plan, Iran will only engage in production of centrifuges, including centrifuge rotors suitable for isotope separation or any other centrifuge components, to meet the enrichment and enrichment R&D requirements of this Annex.

62. Consistent with its plan, Iran will use the stock of IR-1 centrifuge machines in storage, which are in excess of the remaining 5060 IR-1 centrifuges in Natanz and the IR-1 centrifuges installed at Fordow, for the replacement of failed or damaged machines.

63. Consistent with its plan, at the end of year 8, Iran will commence manufacturing of IR-6 and IR-8 centrifuges without rotors through year 10 at a rate of up to 200 centrifuges per year for each type. After year 10, Iran will produce complete centrifuges with the same rate to meet its enrichment and enrichment R&D needs. Iran will store them at Natanz in an above ground location, under IAEA continuous monitoring, until they are needed for final assembly according to the enrichment and enrichment R&D plan.

L. **Additional protocol and modified code 3.1**

64. Iran will notify the IAEA of provisional application of the Additional Protocol to its Safeguards Agreement in accordance with Article 17(b) of the Additional Protocol pending its entry into force, and subsequently seek ratification and entry into force, consistent with the respective roles of the President and the Majli (Parliament).

65. Iran will notify the IAEA that it will fully implement the Modified Code 3.1 of the Subsidiary Arrangement to Iran's Safeguards Agreement as long as the Safeguards Agreement remains in force.

M. **Past and present issues of Concern**

66. Iran will complete all activities as set out in paragraphs 2, 4, 5, and 6 of the "Roadmap for Clarification of Past and Present Outstanding Issues", as verified by the IAEA in its regular updates by the Director General of the IAEA on the implementation of this Roadmap.

N. **Modern technologies and long term presense of IAEA**

67. For the purpose of increasing the efficiency of monitoring for this JCPOA, for 15 years or longer, for the specified verification measures:

67.1. Iran will permit the IAEA the use of on-line enrichment measurement and electronic seals which communicate their status within nuclear sites to IAEA inspectors, as well as other IAEA approved and certified modern technologies in line with internationally accepted IAEA practice. Iran will facilitate automated collection of IAEA measurement recordings registered by installed measurement devices and sending to IAEA working space in individual nuclear sites.

67.2. Iran will make the necessary arrangements to allow for a long-term IAEA presence, including issuing long-term visas, as well as providing proper working space at nuclear sites and, with best efforts, at locations near nuclear sites in Iran for the designated IAEA inspectors for working and keeping necessary equipment.

67.3. Iran will increase the number of designated IAEA inspectors to the range of 130-150 within 9 months from the date of the implementation of the JCPOA, and will generally allow the designation of inspectors from nations that have diplomatic relations with Iran, consistent with its laws and regulations.

O. **Transparency related to uranium Ore Concentrate (UOC)**

68. Iran will permit the IAEA to monitor, through agreed measures that will include containment and surveillance measures, for 25 years, that all uranium ore concentrate produced in Iran or obtained from any other source, is transferred to the uranium conversion facility (UCF) in Esfahan or to any other future uranium conversion facility which Iran might decide to build in Iran within this period.

69. Iran will provide the IAEA with all necessary information such that the IAEA will be able to verify the production of the uranium ore concentrate and the inventory of uranium ore concentrate produced in Iran or obtained from any other source for 25 years.

P. **Transparency related to enrichment**

70. For 15 years, Iran will permit the IAEA to implement continuous monitoring, including through containment and surveillance measures, as necessary, to verify that stored centrifuges and infrastructure remain in storage, and are only used to replace failed or damaged centrifuges, as specified in this Annex.

71. Iran will permit the IAEA regular access, including daily access as requested by the IAEA, to relevant buildings at Natanz, including all parts of the FEP and PFEP, for 15 years.

72. For 15 years, the Natanz enrichment site will be the sole location for all of Iran's uranium enrichment related activities including safeguarded R&D.

73. Iran intends to apply nuclear export policies and practices in line with the internationally established standards for the export of nuclear material, equipment and technology. For 15 years, Iran will only engage, including through export of any enrichment or enrichment related equipment and technology, with any other country, or with any foreign entity in enrichment or enrichment related activities, including related research and development activities, following approval by the Joint Commission.

Q. **Access**

74. Requests for access pursuant to provisions of this JCPOA will be made in good faith, with due observance of the sovereign rights of Iran, and kept to the minimum necessary to effectively implement the verification responsibilities under this JCPOA. In line with normal international safeguards practice, such requests will not be aimed at interfering with Iranian military or other national security activities, but will be exclusively for resolving concerns regarding fulfillment of the JCPOA commitments and Iran's other non-proliferation and safeguards obligations. The following procedures

are for the purpose of JCPOA implementation between the E3/EU+3 and Iran and are without prejudice to the safeguards agreement and the Additional Protocol thereto. In implementing this procedure as well as other transparency measures, the IAEA will be requested to take every precaution to protect commercial, technological and industrial secrets as well as other confidential information coming to its knowledge.

75. In furtherance of implementation of the JCPOA, if the IAEA has concerns regarding undeclared nuclear materials or activities, or activities inconsistent with the JCPOA, at locations that have not been declared under the comprehensive safeguards agreement or Additional Protocol, the IAEA will provide Iran the basis for such concerns and request clarification.

76. If Iran's explanations do not resolve the IAEA's concerns, the Agency may request access to such locations for the sole reason to verify the absence of undeclared nuclear materials and activities or activities inconsistent with the JCPOA at such locations. The IAEA will provide Iran the reasons for access in writing and will make available relevant information.

77. Iran may propose to the IAEA alternative means of resolving the IAEA's concerns that enable the IAEA to verify the absence of undeclared nuclear materials and activities or activities inconsistent with the JCPOA at the location in question, which should be given due and prompt consideration.

78. If the absence of undeclared nuclear materials and activities or activities inconsistent with the JCPOA cannot be verified after the implementation of the alternative arrangements agreed by Iran and the IAEA, or if the two sides are unable to reach satisfactory arrangements to verify the absence of undeclared nuclear materials and activities or activities inconsistent with the JCPOA at the

specified locations within 14 days of the IAEA's original request for access, Iran, in consultation with the members of the Joint Commission, would resolve the IAEA's concerns through necessary means agreed between Iran and the IAEA. In the absence of an agreement, the members of the Joint Commission, by consensus or by a vote of 5 or more of its 8 members, would advise on the necessary means to resolve the IAEA's concerns. The process of consultation with, and any action by, the members of the Joint Commission would not exceed 7 days, and Iran would implement the necessary means within 3 additional days.

R. Centrifuge component manufacturing transparency

79. Iran and the IAEA will take the necessary steps for containment and surveillance on centrifuge rotor tubes and bellows for 20 years.

80. In this context:
80.1. Iran will provide the IAEA with an initial inventory of all existing centrifuge rotor tubes and bellows and subsequent reports on changes in such inventory and will permit the IAEA to verify the inventory by item counting and numbering, and through containment and surveillance, of all rotor tubes and bellows, including in all existing and newly produced centrifuges.

80.2. Iran will declare all locations and equipment, namely flow-forming machines, filament-winding machines and mandrels that are used for production of centrifuge rotor tubes or bellows, and will permit the IAEA to implement continuous monitoring, including through containment and surveillance on this equipment, to verify that this equipment is being used to manufacture centrifuges only for the activities specified in this JCPOA.

S. Other uranium isotope separation activities

81. For 10 years, Iran's uranium isotope separation-related research

and development or production activities will be exclusively based on gaseous centrifuge technology.2 Iran will permit IAEA access to verify that uranium isotope separation production and R&D activities are consistent with this Annex. 2 For the purpose of this Annex, non-gaseous centrifuge uranium isotope separation-related research and development or production will include laser isotope separation systems, electromagnetic isotope separation systems, chemical exchange systems, gaseous diffusion systems, vortex and aerodynamic systems, and other such processes that separate uranium isotopes.

T. Activities which could contribute to the design and development of a nuclear explosive device

82. Iran will not engage in the following activities which could contribute to the development of a nuclear explosive device:

82.1. Designing, developing, acquiring, or using computer models to simulate nuclear explosive devices.

82.2. Designing, developing, fabricating, acquiring, or using multi-point explosive detonation systems suitable for a nuclear explosive device, unless approved by the Joint Commission for non-nuclear purposes and subject to monitoring.

82.3. Designing, developing, fabricating, acquiring, or using explosive diagnostic systems (streak cameras, framing cameras and flash x-ray cameras) suitable for the development of a nuclear explosive device, unless approved by the Joint Commission for non-nuclear purposes and subject to monitoring.

82.4. Designing, developing, fabricating, acquiring, or using explosively driven neutron sources or specialized materials for explosively driven neutron sources.

CHAPTER FOUR

Content of Annex V

Civil Nuclear Cooperation
A. General
1. Iran and E3/EU+3 decided to co-operate, among others, including through IAEA technical cooperation, where appropriate, and without prejudice to the existing bilateral agreements, in different areas of civil nuclear co-operation to be developed within the framework of this JCPOA, as detailed in this Annex. In this context, the Joint Commission will also support assistance to Iran, including through IAEA technical cooperation projects, as appropriate.

2. All civil nuclear cooperation projects under this JCPOA will be mutually determined by the participating states and will be consistent with the JCPOA and the national laws and regulations of the participating parties.

3. The civil nuclear and scientific cooperation projects envisioned between Iran and the E3/EU+3 as part of this JCPOA may be undertaken in a variety of formats, with a variety of potential participants. A given project undertaken by the E3/EU+3 will not necessarily include participation by all E3/EU+3 parties:

3.1. Bilateral or multilateral cooperation arrangements with Iran. Such arrangements would be mutually determined by the participating states.

3.2. Projects under the auspices of the IAEA, either through IAEA technical co-operation projects including through Project and Supply Agreements.

3.3. through International Science and Technology Centres. Specifically, E3/EU+3 parties will undertake to develop nuclear co-operation with Iran, in particular within the following areas:

B. **Reactors, Fuels and Associated Technologies, Facilities and Processes**
4. Modern light water power and research reactors and associated equipment, technology and facilitiesE3/EU+3 parties, as appropriate, will facilitate Iran's acquisition of light-water research and power reactors, for research, development and testing, and for the supply of electricity and desalination, with arrangements for the assured supply of nuclear fuel and the removal of spent fuel as provided for in relevant contracts, for each reactor provided. This may include the following areas for co-operation:

4.1. Construction as well as effective and safe operation of new light water power reactors and associated equipment, according to Generation III+ requirements, including small and medium sized nuclear reactors, including joint design and manufacturing, as appropriate.

4.2. Construction of state of the art light water moderated multipurpose research reactors capable of testing fuel pins, assembly prototypes and structural materials with associated related facilities, including joint design and manufacturing, as appropriate.

4.3. Supply of state-of-the-art instrumentation and control systems for the above research and power reactors, including joint design and manufacturing, as appropriate;

4.4. Supply of nuclear simulation and calculation codes and software solutions with regard to the above areas, including joint development, as appropriate;

4.5. Supply of first and second loop main equipment as well as core of the above research and power reactors, including joint design and manufacturing, as appropriate;

4.6. On-the-job training on fuel management scenarios and reshuffling for the above research and power nuclear reactors;

4.7. Joint technical review of Iran's current nuclear reactors, upon the request by Iran, in order to upgrade current equipment and systems, including concerning nuclear safety;

5. Arak Modernisation Project

5.1. As described in Section B of Annex I, an international partnership composed of E3/EU+3 parties and Iran, which may subsequently be enlarged to include mutually determined third countries will be established, to support and facilitate the redesign and rebuilding of the IR-40 reactor at Arak into a modernised, not exceeding 20MWth, heavy-water moderated and cooled research reactor, based on the agreed conceptual design (as attached to Annex I).

5.2. Iran will take the leadership role as the owner and as the project manager, and have responsibility for overall implementation of the Arak modernisation project. A Working Group composed of E3/EU+3 participants will be established to support and facilitate the redesigning and rebuilding the reactor.
An international partnership composed of Iran and the Working

Group would implement the Arak modernisation project, with E3/EU+3 participants assuming responsibilities as described in Annex I. The Working Group could be enlarged to include other countries by consensus of the participants of the Working Group and Iran. E3/EU+3 participants and Iran will conclude an official document expressing their strong commitments to the Arak modernisation project in advance of Implementation Day which would provide an assured path forward to modernize the reactor and would define the responsibilities assumed by the E3/EU+ participants, especially in the key areas such as redesign, design review and certification, reactor core manufacturing, fuel design, fabrication and supply, safety and security, spent fuel treatment or disposition, as well as concerning the supply of materials, equipment, instrumentation and control systems, and subsequently contracts would be concluded. The participants of the Working Group will provide assistance needed by Iran for redesigning and rebuilding the reactor, consistent with their respective national laws, in such a manner as to enable the safe and timely construction and commissioning of the modernised reactor.

5.3. Iran and the Working Group will cooperate to develop the final design of the modernised reactor and the design of the subsidiary laboratories to be carried out by Iran, and review conformity with international safety standards, such that the reactor can be licensed by the relevant Iranian regulatory authority for commissioning and operation.

5.4. Iran will continue to assume the primary responsibility for financing the modernisation project. Additional funding arrangements for the project, including for IAEA projects supporting the Arak modernisation project, will be determined based on the official document and contracts to be subsequently concluded.

6. **Nuclear Fuel**

6.1. E3/EU+3 parties, as appropriate, will support assistance to Iran, including through the IAEA, as appropriate, in meeting international qualification standards for nuclear fuel fabricated by Iran.

6.2. E3/EU+3 parties will seek to cooperate regarding the supply of modern fuels, including, as appropriate, joint design and fabrication, the relevant licenses and fabrication technologies and equipment and related infrastructure, for current and future nuclear research and power reactors, including technical assistance on purification processes, forming and metallurgical activities for different types of nuclear fuel clads and cladding for the modernised Arak heavy water research reactor.

C. **Research and Development (R&D) Practices**
7. To implement other aspects of this JCPOA and in support of a broader opening of scientific engagements between the E3/EU+3 and Iran, the E3/EU+3 and Iran will seek cooperation and scientific exchange in the field of nuclear science and technology:

7.1. Accelerator-based nuclear physics and nuclear astrophysics research, and stable isotope production in international collaboration at the nuclear, physics, and technology centre at the Fordow facility. Iran will request from the E3/EU+3 and other interested parties' specific proposals for cooperative international nuclear, physics, and technology projects and will host an international workshop to review these proposals. The goal is to realise international collaborative projects within a few years. The transitioning to stable isotope production of two cascades will be conducted in a joint partnership between the Russian Federation and Iran on the basis of arrangements to be mutually agreed upon.
7.2. Plasma physics and nuclear fusion;

7.3. Research reactor applications at the TRR, modernized Arak reactor, or at other future research reactors in Iran, such as:

7.3.1. Training

7.3.2. Radio-isotope production and utilization

7.3.3. Nuclear desalination

7.3.4. Neutron transmutation doping

7.3.5. Neutron activation analysis

7.3.6. Neutron capture therapy

7.3.7. Neutron imaging and materials characterization studies using neutron beams

7.4. E3/EU+3 parties and Iran could also explore co-operation in the following additional areas:

7.4.1. Design, manufacture and/or assembly of in-core measuring instrumentation and technologies;

7.4.2. Nuclear instrumentation and control, systems and electronic design, manufacture and/or assembly;

7.4.3. Fusion technology and plasma physics and related infrastructure and facilitating contribution of Iran to the International Thermonuclear Experimental Reactor (ITER) Project and/or similar projects, including relevant IAEA technical cooperation projects;

7.4.4. Neutrino astronomy;

7.4.5. Design and manufacturing, and supply, of different types of accelerators and supply of related equipment including through relevant IAEA technical cooperation projects;

7.4.6. Data acquisition and processing software and interface equipment;

D. **Nuclear Safety, Safeguards and Security**

8. Nuclear safety E3/EU+3 parties, and possibly other states, as appropriate, are prepared to cooperate with Iran to establish a Nuclear Safety Centre in Iran, engage in workshops and training events in Iran to support interactions between Iranian nuclear regulatory authorities and those from the E3/EU+3 and elsewhere to,

among other things, share lessons learned on establishing and maintaining regulatory independence and effectiveness, and training on implementing nuclear safety culture and best practices; facilitate exchanges and   visits to nuclear regulatory authorities and nuclear power plants outside of Iran focusing on best practices for safe operation; and enhance and strengthen domestic emergency preparedness and severe accident management capability. Provide support and assistance to enable Iran to join relevant conventions on nuclear safety and security, e.g. through workshops or seminars furthering accession to such commitments. Such workshops or seminars could also take place under the auspices of the IAEA. E3/EU+3 parties, and possibly other states, as appropriate, will co-operate with Iran in the following areas of nuclear safety, as well as in other areas to be mutually agreed:

8.1. Conclusion of bilateral/multilateral agreements with related organisations and research centres;

8.2. Supply of valid codes, instruments and equipment related to nuclear safety;

8.3. Facilitate exchange of knowledge and experience in the area of nuclear safety;

8.4. Enhance and strengthen domestic emergency preparedness and severe accident management capability;

8.5. Arrange on-the-job training and apprenticeship courses for reactor and facility operators, regulatory authority personnel and related supportive organizations in the area of nuclear safety inside and outside of Iran;

8.6. Establish a Nuclear Safety Centre in Iran, which shall be equipped with necessary tools, techniques and equipment, in order to support and facilitate technical and professional training and exchange of lessons-learned for reactor and facility operators, regulatory authority personnel and related supportive organizations;

9. Nuclear Safeguards

E3/EU+3 parties, and possibly other states, as appropriate, are prepared to cooperate with Iran on the effective and efficient implementation of IAEA safeguards and transparency measures in Iran. Co-operation in the following areas can be envisaged:

9.1. Cooperation in the form of on-the-job trainings and workshops to strengthen nuclear material accounting and control process, human resource development, and quality assurance/quality control processes;

9.2. E3/EU+3 parties, and other states, as appropriate, are prepared to cooperate with Iran for the effective and efficient implementation of IAEA safeguards and transparency measures in Iran.

9.3. This cooperation could take the form of training and workshops to strengthen Iran's safeguards regulatory authority, nuclear material accounting and control processes, human resource development, and quality assurance/quality control processes.

10. Nuclear Security

E3/EU+3 parties, and possibly other states, as appropriate, are prepared to cooperate with Iran on the implementation of nuclear security guidelines and best practices. Co-operation in the following areas can be envisaged:

10.1. Co-operation in the form of training courses and workshops to strengthen Iran's ability to prevent, protect and respond to nuclear security threats to nuclear facilities and systems as well as to enable effective and sustainable nuclear security and physical protection systems;

10.2. Co-operation through training and workshops to strengthen Iran's ability to protect against, and respond to nuclear security threats, including sabotage, as well as to enable effective and sustainable nuclear security and physical protection systems.

E. **Nuclear Medicine and Radioisotopes, Associated Technologies, Facilities and Processes**

11. E3/EU+3 parties, as appropriate, are prepared to cooperate with Iran to improve the utilization of nuclear medicine in Iran in order to enhance Iran's expertise in diagnostic imaging and radiotherapy, increase the availability of medical radioisotopes for diagnosis and treatment of Iranian citizens, and facilitate Iran's participation in the broader international scientific and nuclear medicine community. Such cooperation may include:

11.1. Upgrades to the infrastructure associated with existing cyclotron facilities, including for medical radioisotopes production.

11.2. Facilitating Iranian acquisition of a new cyclotron, and associated radio-pharmacy equipment, for medical radioisotopes production.

11.3. Acquisition of state-of-the-art diagnostic imaging and radiotherapy equipment for existing or new nuclear medicine centers, including co-operation between hospitals for the treatment of individual patients.

11.4. Cooperation on occupational and patient dosimeter procedures.

11.5. Improved target utilization to increase radioisotope production.

11.6. Acquisition of radioisotope sources for bracho therapy, and radiotherapy instrument calibration, and other medical and industrial applications.

11.7. Supply of state-of-the art radio-medicine center and necessary laboratories.

F. Waste Management and Facility Decommissioning

12. E3/EU+3 parties, as appropriate, are prepared to cooperate with Iran in the safe, effective, and efficient management and disposition of nuclear and radiological wastes derived from Iran's nuclear fuel cycle activities and nuclear medicine, radioisotope production and/or consumption activities.

13. E3/EU+3 parties, as appropriate, are prepared to cooperate with Iran in areas of safe, effective, and environmentally friendly best practices for facility decontamination and decommissioning, including co-operation on long term storage facilities for the repository of low and medium level waste.

14. E3/EU+3 parties, as appropriate, are prepared to facilitate exchanges and visits to relevant sites and locations outside of Iran related to effective waste management and best practices.

15. E3/EU+3 parties, as appropriate, will facilitate the supply of appropriate equipment and systems for waste management and depository facilities in Iran.

G. Other projects

16. Other projects may be implemented between the relevant E3/EU+3 parties and Iran, as mutually determined by the participants in the JCPOA, including in the following areas:

16.1. Construction of nuclear desalination and associated infrastructure in Iran;

16.2. Development of laser technology for medical applications (e.g. for eye surgery).

CHAPTER FIVE

Detailed Content of Annex VI

Joint Commission
1. Establishment, Composition, and Coordinator

1.1. The Joint Commission is established to carry out the functions assigned to it in the JCPOA, including its Annexes.

1.2. The Joint Commission is comprised of representatives of Iran and the E3/EU+3 (China, France, Germany, the Russian Federation, the United Kingdom, and the United States, with the High Representative of the Union for Foreign Affairs and Security Policy), together, the JCPOA participants.

1.3. The Joint Commission may establish Working Groups in particular areas, as appropriate.

1.4. The High Representative of the Union for Foreign Affairs and Security Policy ('High Representative'), or his/her designated representative will serve as the Coordinator of the Joint Commission.

2. Functions
2.1. The Joint Commission will perform the following functions:

2.1.1. Review and approve the final design for the modernized heavy water research reactor and the design of the subsidiary laboratories prior to the commencement of construction, and review and approve the fuel design for the modernized heavy water research reactor as provided for in Section B of Annex I;

2.1.2. Review and approve, upon request by Iran, development, acquisition, construction or operation of hot cells (containing a cell or interconnected cells), shielded cells or shielded glove boxes with dimensions beyond 6 cubic meters in volume and specifications set out in Annex I of the Additional Protocol, as provided for in paragraph 21 of Annex I;

2.1.3. Review and approve plans submitted by Iran to initiate R&D on uranium metal based TRR fuel, as provided for in paragraph 26 of Annex I;

2.1.4. Review and approve, upon request by Iran, projects on new types of centrifuges to proceed to a prototype stage for mechanical testing, as provided for in paragraph 43 of Annex I;

2.1.5. Receive information in advance about the specific projects that will be undertaken at Fordow, as provided for in paragraph 44 of Annex I;

2.1.6. Receive information about the conceptual framework of stable isotope production at Fordow, as provided for in paragraph 46.1 of Annex I;

2.1.7. Assess and then approve, upon request by Iran, that fuel assemblies manufactured in Iran and their intermediate products cannot be readily reconverted into UF6, based on the objective technical criteria, with the goal of enabling fuel to be fabricated in Iran, as provided in paragraph 59 of Annex I;

2.1.8. Support assistance to Iran, including through IAEA technical cooperation as appropriate, in meeting international qualification standards for nuclear fuel produced by Iran, as provided for in paragraph 59 of Annex I;

2.1.9. Review and approve in advance, upon request by Iran, engagement by Iran, including through export of any enrichment or enrichment related equipment and technology, with any other country, or with any foreign entity in enrichment and enrichment related activities, including related research and development, as provided for in paragraph 73 in Annex I;

2.1.10. Provide consultation, and advise on the necessary means in the context of access as specified in paragraph 78 of Annex I;

2.1.11. Review and approve in advance, upon request by Iran, the design, development, fabrication, acquisition, or use for non-nuclear purposes of multi-point explosive detonation systems suitable for a nuclear explosive device and explosive diagnostic systems (streak cameras, framing cameras and flash x-ray cameras) suitable for the development of a nuclear explosive device, as provided for in paragraphs 82.2 and 82.3 of Annex I;

2.1.12. Review and consult to address issues arising from the implementation of sanctions lifting as specified in this JCPOA and its Annex II;

2.1.13. Review and decide on proposals for nuclear-related transfers to or activities with, Iran, in accordance with Section 6 of this Annex and the United Nations Security Council resolution endorsing this JCPOA;

2.1.14. Review, with a view to resolving, any issue that a JCPOA participant believes constitutes nonperformance by another JCPOA participant of its commitments under the JCPOA, according to the process outlined in the JCPOA;

2.1.15. Adopt or modify, as necessary, procedures to govern its activities;

2.1.16. Consult and provide guidance on other implementation matters that may arise under the JCPOA.

3. Procedures

3.1. The Joint Commission will meet on a quarterly basis and at any time upon request of a JCPOA participant to the Coordinator.

The Coordinator will convene a meeting of the Joint Commission to be held no later than one week following receipt of such a request, except for consultations in accordance with Section Q of Annex I and any other matter that the

Coordinator and/or a JCPOA participant deem urgent, in which case the meeting will be convened as soon as possible and not later than three calendar days from receipt of the request.

3.2. Meetings of the Joint Commission will be held in New York, Vienna, or Geneva as appropriate. The host country should facilitate entry formalities for those attending such meetings.

3.3. The Joint Commission may decide by consensus to invite observers to attend its meetings.

3.4. Except as provided in Section 6 of this Annex which will be subject to the confidentiality procedure of the UN, the work of the Joint Commission is confidential and may be shared only among JCPOA participants and observers as appropriate, unless the Joint Commission decides otherwise.

4. Decisions

4.1. Except as stated otherwise in this Annex, decisions by the Joint Commission are to be made by consensus.

4.2. Each JCPOA participant will have one vote. Decisions of the Joint Commission are to be taken by the Representative or the Deputy Representative or other such alternate as the JCPOA participant may designate.

4.3. The vote of each JCPOA participant will be made known to all other JCPOA participants if any JCPOA participant requests a recorded vote.

4.4. Matters before the Joint Commission pursuant to Section Q of Annex I are to be decided by consensus or by affirmative vote of five JCPOA participants. There is no quorum requirement.

4.5. The Coordinator will not take part in decision-making on nuclear-related transfers and activities as set out in Section 6 of this Annex.

5. Other
5.1. Each JCPOA participant will be responsible for its own costs of participating in the Joint Commission, unless the Joint Commission decides otherwise.

5.2. JCPOA participants may request that the Coordinator circulates a notification to the other JCPOA participants at any time. Upon such a request, the Coordinator will circulate such notification without delay to all JCPOA participants.

6. Procurement Working Group
6.1. With the purpose of establishing a procurement channel, the Joint Commission will, except as otherwise provided by the United Nations Security Council resolution endorsing this JCPOA, review and decide on proposals by states seeking to engage in:

6.1.1 The supply, sale or transfer directly or indirectly from their territories, or by their nationals or using their flag vessels or aircraft to, or for the use in or benefit of, Iran, and whether or not originating in their territories, of all items, materials, equipment, goods and technology set out in INFCIRC/254/Rev.12/Part 1, and, if the end-use will be for Iran's nuclear programme set out in this JCPOA or other non-nuclear civilian end-use, all items, materials, equipment, goods and technology set out in INFCIRC/254/Rev.9/Part 2 (or the most recent version of these documents as updated by the Security Council), as well as any further items if the relevant State determines that they could contribute to activities inconsistent with the JCPOA;

6.1.2. the provision to Iran of any technical assistance or training, financial assistance, investment, brokering or other services related

to the supply, sale, transfer, manufacture, or use of the items, materials, equipment, goods and technology.

6.1.3. Acquisition by Iran of an interest in a commercial activity in another State involving uranium mining, production or use of nuclear materials and technologies as listed in INFCIRC/254/Rev.12/Part 1, and such investments in territories under their jurisdiction by Iran, its nationals, and entities incorporated in Iran or subject to its jurisdiction, or by individuals or entities acting on their behalf or direction, or by entities owned or controlled by them.

6.2. The Joint Commission will discharge its responsibility for reviewing and making recommendations on proposals for nuclear-related transfers to or activities with Iran through a Procurement Working Group.

6.3. Each E3+3 State and Iran will participate in the Procurement Working Group. The High Representative will serve as the Coordinator of the Procurement Working Group.

6.4. Except as otherwise provided by the Joint Commission or the United Nations Security Council resolution endorsing this JCPOA, the Procurement Working Group will consider proposals according to the following process:

6.4.1. Upon receipt of a proposal, including all necessary supporting information, by a State seeking to engage in transfers and activities referenced in Section 6.1, the Coordinator will forward the proposal, through appropriate means, without delay to the Procurement Working Group and, when the proposal relates to items, material, equipment, goods and technology intended to be used in nuclear activities authorized by the JCPOA, to the IAEA.
The Procurement Working Group will have up to 30 working days to consider and decide on the proposal.

6.4.2. "Necessary supporting information" for purposes of Section 6.4.1 means: (a) a description of the item; (b) the name, address, telephone number, and email address of the exporting entity; (c) the name, address, telephone number, and email address of the importing entity; (d) a statement of the proposed end-use and end use location, along with an end-use certification signed by the AEOI or the appropriate authority of Iran attesting the stated end-use; (e) export license number if available; (f) contract date, if available; and (g) details on transportation, if available; provided that if any of the export license number, contract date, or details on transportation are not available as of the time of submittal of the proposal, such information will be provided as soon as possible and in any event as condition of approval prior to shipment of the item.

6.4.3. Each participant in the Procurement Working Group will have to communicate to the Coordinator, within 20 working days, whether it approves or rejects the proposal. The timeline for consideration may be extended for an additional period of 10 working days at the request of a participant of the Procurement Working Group.

6.4.4. The proposal will be recommended for approval as soon as the Coordinator receives formal approvals from all the Procurement Working Group Participants or if, at the end of the 30 working day period, the Coordinator has received no disapprovals from any of the Procurement Working Group Participants. If at the end of the 30 working day period, the proposal has not been recommended for approval, the proposal may, at the request of at least two Working Group Participants within 5 working days, be referred to the Joint Commission, which would decide on approval of the proposal by consensus within 10 working days.

Otherwise the proposal will be recommended for disapproval. The disapproving JCPOA participant(s) should provide relevant information regarding the disapproval to the Joint Commission as appropriate, taking into account the need to protect confidential information.

6.4.5. The Coordinator will communicate the recommendation of the Joint Commission to the United Nations Security Council no later than 35 working days, or in case of referral to the Joint Commission no later than 45 working days from the date the Coordinator transmitted the proposal and all necessary supporting information to the Procurement Working Group.

6.4.6. Except as decided otherwise by consensus, the Procurement Working Group will meet every three weeks for reviewing the proposals. When some of the proposals to be reviewed relate to items, material, equipment, goods and technology intended to be used in nuclear activities authorized by the JCPOA, the IAEA may be invited to attend the meeting as an observer.

6.5. All JCPOA participants will act in accordance with the procurement channel and will only engage in transfers and activities referenced in Section 6.1 following approval by the Joint Commission and the United Nations Security Council. Iran will not use, acquire, or seek to procure the items, materials, equipment, goods, and technology referred to in Section 6.1 of this Annex for nuclear activities which are inconsistent with this JCPOA.

6.6. Any JCPOA participant may refer a procurement-related activity to the Joint Commission under the dispute settlement mechanism if it is concerned that such activity is inconsistent with this JCPOA.

6.7. Iran will provide to the IAEA access to the locations of intended use of all items, materials, equipment, goods and technology set out in INFCIRC/254/Rev.12/Part 1 (or the most recent version of these documents as updated by the Security Council) imported following the procedure under Section 6 of this Annex.

6.8. Iran will permit the exporting state to verify the end-use of all items, materials, equipment, goods and technology set out in INFCIRC/254/Rev.9/Part 2 (or the most recent version of these documents as updated by the Security Council) imported following the procedure under Section 6 of this Annex. Upon request of the exporting state, or if the Joint Commission deems necessary when approving a proposal for transfer, the Joint Commission will provide expertise to the exporting state, including experts, as needed, to participate in the end-use verification.

6.9. The Procurement Working Group will respond to requests for guidance on procurement activities from third parties, as communicated by the Coordinator. The Procurement Working Group will endeavor to respond to such requests for guidance within 9 working days from the date the Coordinator submits it to the Procurement Working Group.

6.10. The Joint Commission will report to the United Nations Security Council at least every 6 months on the status of the Procurement Working Group's decisions and on any implementation issues.

7. Working Group on Implementation of Sanctions Lifting
7.1. The Joint Commission will discharge its responsibilities for reviewing and consulting on issues related to the implementation of sanctions lifting as specified in this JCPOA assisted by a working group on the implementation of sanctions lifting.

7.2. The Joint Commission participants will participate in this working group. The High Representative will serve as coordinator of this working group.

7.3. If at any time following the implementation day Iran believes that any other nuclear related sanction or restrictive measure including related designations of the E3/EU+3 is preventing the full implementation of the sanctions lifting as specified in this JCPOA, the JCPOA participant in question will consult with Iran with a view to resolving the issue. If they are not able to resolve the issue, Iran or any member of the E3/EU+3 may refer the issue to the working group.

7.4. The participants of the working group will review and consult, with a view to resolving the issue within 30 working days.

7.5. If after involvement of the working group, the issue remains unresolved, any participant of the JCPOA may refer it to the Joint Commission.

CHAPTER SIX

Important Facts about the Iran Deal

Summary of the Deal

Major provisions of the final accord include the following: Iran's current stockpile of low-enriched uranium will be reduced by 98 percent, from 10,000 kg to 300 kg. This reduction will be maintained for fifteen years. For the same fifteen-year period, Iran will be limited to enriching uranium to 3.67%, a percentage sufficient for civilian nuclear power and research, but not for building a nuclear weapon. However, the number of centrifuges is sufficient for a nuclear weapon, but not for nuclear power. This is a "major decline in Iran's previous nuclear activity; prior to watering down its stockpile pursuant to the Joint Plan of Action interim agreement, Iran had enriched uranium to near 20% (medium-enriched uranium). This enriched uranium in excess of 300 kg of up to 3.67% will be down blended to natural uranium level or be sold in return for natural uranium, and the uranium enriched to between 5% and 20% will be fabricated into fuel plates for the Tehran Research Reactor or sold or diluted to an enrichment level of 3.67%. The implementation of the commercial contracts will be facilitated by P5+1. After fifteen years, all physical limits on enrichment will be removed, including limits on the type and number of centrifuges, Iran's stockpile of enriched uranium, and the where Iran may have enrichment facilities. At this point Iran could expand its nuclear program to create more practical overt and covert nuclear weapons options.

For ten years, Iran will place over two-thirds of its centrifuges in storage, from its current stockpile of 19,000 centrifuges (of which 10,000 were operational) to no more than 6,104 operational centrifuges, with only 5,060 allowed to enrich uranium, with the enrichment capacity being limited to the Natanz plant. The centrifuges there must be IR-1 centrifuges, the first-generation centrifuge type which is Iran's oldest and least efficient; Iran will give up its advanced IR-2M centrifuges in this period. The non- operating centrifuges will be stored in Natanz and monitored by IAEA, but may be used to replace failed centrifuges. Iran will not build any new uranium-enrichment facilities for fifteen years. Iran may continue research and development work on enrichment, but that work will take place only at the Natanz facility and include certain limitations for the first eight years. This is intended to keep the country to a breakout time of one year.

Iran, with cooperation from the "*Working Group*" (the P5+1 and possibly other countries), will modernise and rebuild the Arak heavy water research reactor based on an agreed design to support its peaceful nuclear research and production needs and purposes, but in such a way to minimise the production of plutonium and not to produce weapons-grade plutonium. The power of the redesigned reactor will not exceed 20 MWth. The P5+1 parties will support and facilitate the timely and safe construction of the Arak complex. All spent fuel will be sent out of the country. All excess heavy water which is beyond Iran's needs for the redesigned reactor will be made available for export to the international market based on international prices.

For 15 years, Iran will not engage in, or research on, spent fuel reprocessing. Iran will also not build any additional heavy-water reactors or accumulate heavy water for fifteen years Iran's Fordow facility will stop enriching uranium and researching uranium enrichment for at least fifteen years; the facility will be converted into a nuclear physics and technology center. For 15 years, Fordow will maintain no more than 1,044 IR-1 centrifuges in six cascades in one wing of Fordow. *"Two of those six cascades will spin without uranium and will be transitioned, including through appropriate infrastructure modification,"* for stable radioisotope production for medical, agricultural, industrial, and scientific use. "The other four cascades with all associated infrastructure will remain idle." Iran will not be permitted to have any fissile material in Fordow. Iran will implement an Additional Protocol agreement which will continue in perpetuity for as long as Iran remains a party to the Nuclear Non-Proliferation Treaty (NPT). The signing of the Additional Protocol represents a continuation of the monitoring and verification provisions *"long after the comprehensive agreement between the P5+1 and Iran is implemented."* A comprehensive inspections regime will be implemented in order to monitor and confirm that Iran is complying with its obligations and is not diverting any fissile material.

The IAEA will have multilayered oversight "over Iran's entire nuclear supply chain, from uranium mills to its procurement of nuclear-related technologies." For declared nuclear sites such as Fordow and Natanz, the IAEA will have "round-the-clock access" to nuclear facilities and will be entitled to maintain continuous monitoring (including via surveillance equipment) at such sites. The agreement authorizes the IAEA to make use of sophisticated monitoring technology, such as fiber-optic seals on equipment that can electronically send information to the IAEA; infrared satellite imagery to detect covert sites, "environmental sensors that can detect minute signs of nuclear particles"; tamper-resistant, radiation-resistant cameras. Other tools include computerized accounting programs to gather information and detect anomalies, and big data sets on Iranian imports, to monitor dual-use items.

If IAEA inspectors have concerns that Iran is developing nuclear capabilities at any non-declared sites, they may request access "to verify the absence of undeclared nuclear materials and activities or activities inconsistent with" the agreement, informing Iran of the basis for their concerns. The inspectors would only come from countries with which Iran has diplomatic relations. Iran may admit the inspectors to such site or propose alternatives to inspection that might satisfy the IAEA's concerns. If such an agreement cannot be reached, a process running to a maximum of 24 days is triggered. Under this process, Iran and the IAEA have 14 days to resolve disagreements among themselves. If they fail to, the Joint Commission (including all eight parties) would have one week in which to consider the intelligence which initiated the IAEA request. A majority of the Commission (at least five of the eight members) could then inform Iran of the action that it would be required to take within three more days. The majority rule provision "*means the United States and its European allies—Britain, France, Germany and the EU—could insist on access or any other steps and that Iran, Russia or China could not veto them.*" If Iran did not comply with the decision within three days, sanctions would be automatically re-imposed under the snapback provision.

Summary of Sanctions against Iran

The following provisions regarding sanctions are written into the JCPOA: Following the issuance of IAEA report verifying implementation by Iran of the nuclear-related measures, the UN sanctions against Iran and some EU sanctions will terminate and some will be suspended. Once sanctions are lifted, Iran will recover approximately $100 billion of its assets (U.S. Treasury Department estimate) frozen in overseas banks. Eight years into the agreement, EU sanctions against a number of Iranian companies, individuals and institutions (such as the Revolutionary Guards) will be lifted. The U.S. will "cease" application of its nuclear-related secondary sanctions by presidential action or executive waiver. Secondary sanctions are those that sanction other countries for doing business with Iran.

Primary U.S. sanctions, which prohibit U.S. firms from conducting commercial transactions with few exceptions, are not altered by the JCPOA. This step is not tied to any specific date, but is expected to occur "roughly in the first half of 2016." Sanctions relating to ballistic missile technologies would remain for eight years; similar sanctions on conventional weapon sales to Iran would remain for five years. However, all U.S. sanctions against Iran related to alleged human rights abuses, missiles, and support for terrorism are not affected by the agreement and will remain in place. U.S. sanctions are viewed as more stringent, since many have extraterritorial effect (i.e., they apply worldwide). EU sanctions, by contrast, apply only in Europe. No new UN or EU nuclear-related sanctions or restrictive measures will be imposed. If Iran violates the agreement, any of the P5+1 can invoke a "snap back" provision, under which the sanctions "snap back" into place (i.e., are re-implemented). Specifically, the JCPOA establishes the following dispute resolution process:

i. If a party to the JCPOA has reason to believe that another party is not upholding its commitments under the agreement, then the complaining party may refer its complaint to the Joint Commission, a body created under the JCPOA to monitor implementation.

ii. If a complaint made by a non-Iran party is not resolved to the satisfaction of the complaining party within thirty-five days of referral, then that party could treat the unresolved issue as grounds to cease performing its commitments under the JCPOA, notify the United Nations Security Council that it believes the issue constitutes significant non-performance, or both. The Security Council would then have thirty days to adopt a resolution to continue the lifting of sanctions. If such a resolution is not adopted within those thirty days, then the sanctions of all of the pre-JCPOA nuclear-related UN Security Council resolutions would automatically be re-imposed. Iran has stated that in such a case, it would cease performing its nuclear obligations under the deal.
The effect of this rule is that any permanent member of the Security Council (the U.S., Britain, China, Russia and France) can veto any ongoing sanctions relief, but no member can veto the re-imposition of sanctions.

iii. Snapback sanctions would not apply with retroactive effect to contracts signed between any party and Iran or Iranian individuals and entities prior to the date of application, provided that the activities contemplated under and execution of such contracts are consistent with this JCPOA and the previous and current UN Security Council resolutions.

CHAPTER SEVEN

United Nations Security Council

AS provided for in the JCPOA, the agreement was formally endorsed by the UN Security Council, incorporating it into international law. On 15 July 2015, the American ambassador to the UN, Samantha Power, circulated a fourteen-page draft to Council members. On 20 July 2015, the Security Council unanimously approved the fourteen-page resolution—United Nations Security Council resolution in a 15–0 vote. The resolution delays its official implementation for 90 days, to allow for the U.S. Congress' consideration under the Iran Nuclear Agreement Review Act of 2015. The resolution lays out the steps for terminating sanctions imposed by seven past Security Council resolutions, but retains an arms embargo and ballistic missile technology ban. The resolution also did not affect the sanctions imposed separately by the United States and the European Union.

The resolution also codifies the "snapback" mechanism of the agreement, under which all Security Council sanctions will be automatically re-imposed if Iran breaches the deal. Louis Rene Beres, emeritus professor of international law at Purdue University, wrote in The Washington Times that Iranian declarations regarding Israel were *"impermissible in jurisprudence"* and violated the Genocide Convention. The Convention *"criminalizes not only genocide per se"*, but also conspiracy and public incitement to commit genocide and, according to Beres, the Convention as well as all treaties is premised upon the doctrine of *pacta sunt servanda* (Latin for "agreements must be honored"). Thus

Obama administration's failure to enforce anti-genocide norms in its nuclear dealings with Iran constitutes a serious violation of both international and U.S. law. On the same day that the Security Council approved a resolution, the European Union formally approved the JCPOA via a vote of the EU Foreign Affairs Council (the group of EU foreign ministers) meeting in Brussels. This sets into motion the lifting of certain EU sanctions, including those prohibiting the purchase of Iranian oil. The EU continues its sanctions relating to human rights and its sanctions prohibiting the export of ballistic missile technology. The approval by the EU was seen as a signal to the U.S. Congress.

Strategy of the Obama Administration

Under U.S. law, the JCPOA is in the form of an executive agreement. In contrast to treaties, which require two-thirds of the Senate to consent to ratification, executive agreements ordinarily require no congressional approval. Under the terms of the Iran Nuclear Agreement Review Act of 2015, which was signed into law on May 22, 2015, (the agreement underwent a sixty-day review in the United States Congress). Under that Act, once all documents have been sent to the Capitol, Congress will have sixty days in which it can pass a resolution of approval, a resolution of disapproval, or do nothing. (The Act includes additional time beyond the sixty days for the president to veto a resolution and for Congress to take a vote on whether to override or sustain the veto.) During the process sixty days review period process; President Obama said he will veto any resolution of disapproval. Thus, Republicans will only be able to defeat the deal if they can muster the two-thirds of both houses of Congress needed to override a veto of any resolution of disapproval.

This means that 34 votes in the Senate could sustain a veto and place the JCPOA into effect. On July 19, 2015, the State Department officially transmitted to Congress the JCPOA, its annexes, and related materials. These documents include the Unclassified Verification Assessment Report on the JCPOA and the Intelligence Community's Classified Annex to the Verification Assessment Report. The sixty-day review period began the next day, July 20, and ended on September 17 2015. The international community has long sought a landmark diplomatic agreement with Iran on its nuclear program, and such an agreement was also a long-sought foreign-policy goal of the Obama administration. In comments made in the East Room of the White House on 15 July 2015, President Obama urged Congress to support the agreement, saying *"If we don't choose wisely, I believe future generations will judge us harshly, for letting this moment slip away."*

Obama asserted that the inspections regime in the agreement was among the most vigorous ever negotiated and criticized opponents of the deal for failing to offer a viable alternative to it. He stated: *"If 99 percent of the world's community and the majority of nuclear experts look at this thing and they say 'this will prevent Iran from getting a nuclear bomb,' and you are arguing either that it does not ... then you should have some alternative to present. And I haven't heard that."* The same day, Obama made a case for the deal on the agreement in an interview with New York Times columnist Thomas Friedman. Obama stated: *"With respect to Iran, it is a great civilization, but it also has an authoritarian theocracy in charge that is anti-American, anti-Israeli, anti-Semitic, sponsors terrorism, and there are a whole host of real profound differences that we [have with] them... Their argument was, 'We're entitled to have a peaceful nuclear program.'... You know, I have a lot of differences with Ronald Reagan, but where I completely admire him was his recognition that [we] were able to verify an agreement that [was negotiated] with the evil empire [the Soviet Union] that was hell bent on our destruction and was a far greater existential threat to us than Iran will ever be... I had a lot of disagreements with Richard Nixon, but he understood there was the* prospect, the possibility, that China could take a different path. You test these things, and as long as we are preserving our security capacity — as long as we are not giving away our ability to respond forcefully, militarily, where necessary to protect our friends and our allies — that is a risk we have to take. It is a practical, common-sense position. It's not naïve; it's a recognition that if we can in fact resolve some of these differences, without resort to force, that will be a lot better for us and the people of that region."

Also on July 15, Vice President Joe Biden met with Senate Democrats on the Foreign Relations Committee on Capitol Hill, where he made a presentation on the agreement. On July 18, Obama devoted his weekly radio address to the agreement, stating that "*this deal will make America and the world safer and more secure*" and rebutting "*a lot of overheated and often dishonest arguments about it.*" Obama stated "*as commander-in-chief, I make no apology for keeping this country safe and secure through the hard work of diplomacy over the easy rush to war.*"

On July 23, President Obama met in the White House Cabinet Room with about a dozen undecided House Democrats to speak about the agreement and seek their support. The debate over the agreement was marked by acrimony between the White House and with Republicans inside and outside of Congress. Senator Ted Cruz of Texas said that under the agreement would cause "*the Obama administration will become the leading financier of terrorism against America in the world.*" Former Governor Mike Huckabee of Arkansas, a candidate for the Republican presidential nomination, called the president "*naive*" and repeatedly invoked the Holocaust, saying that the president's policy would "*take the Israelis and march them to the door of the oven.*"

At a June 27 news conference, Obama specifically criticized Huckabee, Cruz, and Cotton, saying that such remarks were *"just part of a general pattern we've seen that would be considered ridiculous if it weren't so sad, especially from leaders in the Republican Party."* Obama stated that *"flinging out ad hominem attacks like that ... doesn't help inform the American people"* and stated: *"This is a deal that has been endorsed by people like Brent Scowcroft and Sam Nunn ... historic Democratic and Republican leaders on arms control and on keeping America safe. And so when you get rhetoric like this, maybe it gets attention and maybe this is just an effort to push Mr. Trump out of the headlines, but it's not the kind of leadership that is needed for America right now."*

On August 5, Obama gave a speech before an audience of around 200 at American University, marking a new phase in the administration's campaign for the agreement. Obama stated: *"Let's not mince words: The choice we face is ultimately between diplomacy and some form of war—maybe not tomorrow, maybe not three months from now, but soon. How can we in good conscience justify war before we've tested a diplomatic agreement that achieves our objectives?"* In his speech,

Obama also invoked a speech made by John F. Kennedy at American University in 1963 in favor of the Partial Nuclear Test Ban Treaty. Obama also said that the opponents of the agreement were the same people who created the *"drumbeat of war"* that led to the Iraq War and criticized *"knee-jerk partisanship that has become all too familiar, rhetoric that renders every decision made to be some sort of surrender."*

New York Senator Chuck Schumer, a senior Democrat, made a different assessment of prospects for war by distinguishing between nuclear and non-nuclear aspects of the agreement. In each case he asked whether we are better off with the agreement or without it and his conclusion was: "... when it comes to the nuclear

New York Senator Chuck Schumer, a senior Democrat, made a different assessment of prospects for war by distinguishing between nuclear and non-nuclear aspects of the agreement. In each case he asked whether we are better off with the agreement or without it and his conclusion was: *"... when it comes to the nuclear aspects of the agreement within ten years, we might be slightly better off with it. However, when it comes to the nuclear aspects after ten years and the non-nuclear aspects, we would be better off without it."* Then Schumer assessed the Iranian regime, saying, *"Who's to say this dictatorship will not prevail for another ten, twenty, or thirty years? To me, the very real risk that Iran will not moderate and will, instead, use the agreement to pursue its nefarious goals is too great."* And, finally, Schumer concluded: *"I will vote to disapprove the agreement, not because I believe war is a viable or desirable option, nor to challenge the path of diplomacy. It is because I believe Iran will not change, and under this agreement it will be able to achieve its dual goals of eliminating sanctions while ultimately retaining its nuclear and non-nuclear power."* In the same speech, Obama stated: *"Just because Iranian hard-liners chant 'Death to America' does not mean that that's what all Iranians believe. In fact, it's those hard-liners who are most comfortable with the status quo. It's those hard-liners chanting 'Death to America' who have been most opposed to the deal. They're making common cause with the Republican caucus."* This statement was criticized by congressional Republican leaders. Senate Majority Leader Mitch McConnell called it *"crass political rhetoric"* that was a strategy to *"Demonize your opponents, gin up the base, get the Democrats all angry, and rally around the president."* McConnell said *"This is an enormous national security debate that the president will leave behind, under the Constitution, a year and a half from now, and the rest of us will be dealing with the consequences of it. So I wish he would tone down the rhetoric and let's talk about the facts"* and promised that Republicans would discuss the agreement respectfully in September. Republican Senator Bob Corker, the chairman of Foreign Relations Committee, asserted that the president was *"trying to shut down debate by saying that those who have legitimate questions, legitimate questions — are somehow unpatriotic, are somehow compared to hardliners in Iran."* The president subsequently stood by his statement, with White House Press Secretary Josh Earnest calling it a *"statement of fact"* and the President saying in an interview, *"Remember, what I said was that it's the hard-liners in Iran who are most opposed to this deal. And I said, in that sense, they're making common cause with those who are opposed to this deal here. I didn't say that they were equivalent."* In the same interview, Obama said: *"A sizable proportion of the Republicans were opposed before the ink was even dry on the deal."*

CHAPTER EIGHT

Public Debate on the Deal

An intense public debate in the U.S. took place during the congressional review period. Some of the wealthiest and most powerful donors in American politics, those for and against the accord, became involved in the public debate, although mega-donors opposing the agreement have contributed substantially more money than those supporting it. From 2010 to early August 2015, the foundations of Sheldon Adelson, Paul Singer, and Haim Saban contributed a total of $13 million (at least $7.5 million, at least $2.6 million, and at least $2.9 million, respectively) to advocacy groups opposing an agreement with Iran. On the other side, three groups lobbying in support of the agreement received at least $803,000 from the Ploughshares Fund, at least $425,000 from the Rockefeller Brothers Fund, and at least $68,500 from George Soros and his foundation. Other philanthropists and donors supporting an agreement include S. Daniel Abraham, Tim Gill, Norman Lear, Margery Tabankin, and Arnold Hiatt.

Many Iranian Americans, even those who fled repression in

Iran and oppose the regime there, welcomed the JCPOA as a step forward. The National Iranian American Council (NIAC), Iranian American Bar Association, and other Iranian American organisations welcomed the JCPOA. The NIAC released a statement saying: "*Our negotiators have done their job to win a strong nuclear deal that* c *prevents an Iranian nuclear weapon, all the while avoiding a catastrophic war. Now is the time for Congress to do theirs. Make* no *mistake: if Congress rejects this good deal with Iran, there will be no better deal forthcoming and Congress will be left owning an unnecessary war.*" NIAC created a new group, NIAC Action.

NIAC also organized an open letter from 73 Middle East and foreign affairs scholars stating that *"reactivating diplomatic channels between the United States and* **Iran** *is a necessary first step"* to reduce conflict in the region, and that while *"the nuclear deal will not automatically or immediately bring stability to the region ... Ultimately, a Middle East where diplomacy is the norm rather than the exception will enhance U.S. national security and interests,"* Signatories to the letter include John Esposito, Ehsan Yarshater, Noam Chomsky, Peter Beinart, John Mearsheimer, and Stephen Walt. U.S. pro-Israel groups divided on the JCPOA. The American Israel Public Affairs Committee opposed the agreement, and formed a new *"Citizens for a Nuclear Free Iran"* to run a television advertising campaign against the JCPOA. In August 2015, it was reported that AIPAC and Citizens for a Nuclear Free Iran plan to spend between $20 million and $40 million on its campaign. From mid-July to August 4, 2015, AIPAC's Citizens for a Nuclear Free Iran spent more than $11 million running network television political advertisements opposing the agreement in 23 states, spending more than $1 million in the large states of California, Florida, New York, and Texas. In the first week of August, AIPAC said that it had 400 meetings with congressional offices as part of its campaign to defeat the agreement. In contrast to AIPAC, another pro-Israel organization, J Street, supports the agreement, and plans a $5 million advertising effort of its own to encourage Congress to support the agreement. During the first week of August, J Street launched a $2 million, three-week ad campaign in support of the agreement, with television ads running in Colorado, Maryland, Michigan, Oregon, and Pennsylvania. From mid-July through early August, J Street reported having 125 meetings with congressional offices. J Street has also paid to fly prominent Israelis who support the agreement (including Amram Mitzna, a retired Israeli general, member of the Knesset, and mayor of Haifa) to the U.S. to help persuade members of Congress to support the agreement.

The group United Against Nuclear Iran (UANI) opposed the agreement and committed to spending more than $20 million on a national "TV, radio, print and digital campaign" against the agreement. After UANI announced its opposition, the group's president and co-founder, nonproliferation expert Gary Samore, announced that he had concluded "that the accord was in the United States' interest" and supported the agreement. Samore thus stepped down as president and was replaced by ex-Senator Joseph I. Lieberman. By August 20, UANI had released its third national television ad against the agreement.

On July 17, 2015, a bipartisan open letter endorsing the Iran agreement was signed by more than 100 former U.S. ambassadors and high-ranking State Department officials. The ex-ambassadors wrote: *"If properly implemented, this comprehensive and rigorously negotiated agreement can be an effective instrument in arresting Iran's nuclear program and preventing the spread of nuclear weapons in the volatile and vitally important region of the Middle East. In our judgment the [plan] deserves Congressional support and the opportunity to show it can work. We firmly believe that the most effective way to protect U.S. national security and that of our allies and friends is to ensure that tough-minded diplomacy has a chance to succeed before considering other more costly and risky alternatives."* Among the signatories to the letter were Daniel C. Kurtzer, James Robert Jones, Frank E. Loy, Princeton N. Lyman, Jack F. Matlock, Jr., Donald F. McHenry, Thomas E. McNamara, and Thomas R. Pickering.

A separate public letter to Congress in support of the agreement from five former U.S. ambassadors to Israel from administrations of both parties, and three former Under Secretaries of State was released on July 26, 2015. This letter was signed by R. Nicholas Burns, James B. Cunningham, William C. Harrop, Daniel Kurtzer, Thomas R. Pickering, Edward S. Walker, Jr., and Frank G. The former officials wrote: *"We are persuaded that this agreement will put in place a set of constraints and monitoring measures that will arrest Iran's nuclear program for at least fifteen years and assure that this agreement will leave Iran no legitimate avenue to produce a nuclear weapon during the next ten to fifteen years. This landmark agreement removes the threat that a nuclear-armed Iran would pose to the region and to Israel specifically.*" Another public letter to Congress urging approval of the agreement was signed by a bipartisan group of more than sixty "*national-security leaders*," including politicians, retired military officers, and diplomats. This letter, dated July 20, 2015, stated: "*We congratulate President Obama and all the negotiators for a landmark agreement unprecedented in its importance for preventing the acquisition of nuclear weapons by Iran...We have followed carefully the negotiations as they have progressed and conclude that the JCPOA represents the achievement of greater security for us and our partners in the region*"

On August 8, 2015, 29 prominent U.S. scientists, mostly physicists, published an open letter endorsing the agreement. The letter, addressed to President Obama, said: "*We congratulate you and your team on negotiating a technically sound, stringent and innovative deal that will provide the necessary assurance in the coming decade and more than Iran is not developing nuclear weapons, and provides a basis for further initiates to raise the barriers to nuclear proliferation in the Middle East and around the globe.*" **The letter also stated that the agreement "***will advance the cause of peace and security in the Middle East and can serve as a guidepost for future nonproliferation agreements.*" The 29 signatories included some of the world's most knowledgeable experts in the fields of nuclear weapons and arms control, many of whom have been longtime advisers to Congress, the White House, and federal agencies. Six Nobel Prize in Physics laureates signed the letter: Philip W. Anderson of Princeton University; Leon N. Cooper of Brown University; Sheldon L. Glashow of Boston University; David Gross of the University of California, Santa Barbara; Burton Richter of Stanford University; and Frank Wilczek of the

Massachusetts Institute of Technology. Among the other scientists to sign are Richard L. Garwin (a nuclear physicist who played a key role in the development of the first hydrogen bomb and who was described by the New York Times as *"among the last living physicists who helped usher in the nuclear age"*); Siegfried S. Hecker (a Stanford physicist and the former director of Los Alamos National Laboratory); Rush D. Holt (a physicist and former U.S. Representative who is now the president of the American Association for the Advancement of Science); Freeman Dyson (of Princeton), and Sidney Drell (of Stanford).

On August 11, 2015, an open letter endorsing the agreement signed by 36 retired military generals and admirals, entitled "The Iran Deal Benefits U.S. National Security: An Open Letter from Retired Generals and Admirals was released. The letter, signed by retired officers from all five branches of the U.S. armed services, said that the agreement was *"the most effective means currently available to* **prevent** *Iran from obtaining nuclear weapons,"* **and said that** *"If at* **some** *point it becomes necessary to consider military action against Iran, gathering sufficient international support for such an effort would only be possible if we have first given the diplomatic path a chance. We must exhaust diplomatic options before moving to military ones."* The signers included General James E. Hoss Cartwright of the Marine Corps, former vice chairman of the Joint Chiefs of Staff; General Joseph P. Hoar of the Marine Corps, the former commander of the U.S. Central Command; and Generals Merrill McPeak and Lloyd W. Newton of the Air Force. Other signers include Lieutenant Generals Robert G. Gard, Jr. and Claudia J. Kennedy; Vice Admiral Lee F. Gunn; Rear Admirals Garland Wright and Joseph Sestak; and Major General Paul D. Eaton.

The above letter was answered on August 25, 2016, by a letter signed by nearly 200 retired generals and admirals opposing the deal (the number of signers later rose to 214, with a letter **asserting** that *"The agreement does not 'cut off every pathway' for*

Iran to acquire nuclear weapons. To the contrary, it provides Iran with a legitimate pathway for doing exactly that simply by abiding by the deal." This letter was organized by Leon A. Among those signing the letter were Admiral James A. Lyons; Lieutenant General William G. Boykin, former Undersecretary of Defense for Intelligence; Lieutenant General Thomas McInerney, the retired vice commander of US Air Forces in Europe. The letter said there was no credibility within the agreement's "*inspection process or the ability to snap back sanctions once lifted, should Iran violate the agreement.*", and said that "*In this and other respects, the JCPOA would threaten the national security and vital interests of the United States and, therefore, should be disapproved by the Congress.*" Retired Marine Corps General Anthony Zinni said that he had refused requests from both sides to sign their letters, saying to Time magazine: "*I'm convinced that 90% of the guys who signed the letter one way or the other don't have any clue about whether it's a good or bad deal. They sign it because somebody's asked them to sign it.*" As to the JCPOA, Zinni said: "*The agreement's fine, if you think it can work. But if this is a Neville Chamberlain then you're in a world of shit.*"

On August 13, retired Senators Carl Levin of Michigan, a Democrat, and John Warner of Virginia, a Republican, co-wrote an op-ed in support of the agreement—entitled "*Why hawks should also back the Iran deal*"—published in Politico. Levin and Warner, both past chairmen of the Senate Armed Services Committee, argued that "*If we reject the agreement, we risk isolating ourselves and damaging our ability to assemble the strongest possible coalition to stop Iran*" in the event that military action was needed in the future.

Levin and Warner wrote that "*The deal on the table is a strong agreement on many counts, and it leaves in place the robust deterrence and credibility of a military option. We urge our former colleagues not to take any action which would undermine the deterrent value of a coalition that participates in and could support the use of a military option. The failure of the United States to join the agreement would have that effect.*" Significantly, on August 14, retired senators Richard Lugar of Indiana, a Republican, and J. Bennett Johnston of Louisiana, a Democrat, also wrote in support of the agreement. In a column for Reuters, Lugar and Johnston argued that "*Rejection of the agreement would severely undermine the U.S. role as a leader and reliable partner around the globe. If Washington walks away from this hard-fought multilateral agreement, its dependability would likely be doubted for decades.*" They also wrote: "*Tehran would be the winner of this U.S. rejection because it would achieve its major objective: the lifting of most sanctions without being required to accept constraints on its nuclear program. Iran could also claim to be a victim of American perfidy and try to convince other nations to break with U.S. leadership and with the entire international sanctions regime.*

On August 17, 2015, a group of 75 arms control and nuclear non-proliferation experts issued a joint statement endorsing the agreement. The statement said that "*the JCPOA is a strong, long-term, and verifiable agreement that will be a net-plus for international nuclear nonproliferation efforts*" and that the JCPOA's "*rigorous limits and transparency measures will make it very likely that any future effort by Iran to pursue nuclear weapons, even a clandestine program, would be detected promptly, providing the opportunity to intervene decisively to prevent Iran from acquiring a nuclear weapon.*" The letter was organized through the nonpartisan Arms Control Association. Among the 75 signatories were the Valerie Plame and Joseph C. Wilson; former IAEA director-general Hans Blix; Morton H. Halperin; and experts from the Brookings Institution, Stimson Center, and other think tanks.

Foreign diplomats are also involved in the congressional debate. The Israeli ambassador to the United States Ron Dermer appeared on cable television shows to attack the agreement, while ambassadors from European nations, including Sir Peter Westmacott, the British ambassador to the United States, came on to say the precise opposite. Dermer also lobbied members of Congress on Capitol Hill against the agreement, while diplomats from France, Britain, and Germany made the rounds on Capitol Hill to advocate for the agreement. On August 4, P5+1 diplomats held "*a rare meeting of world powers' envoys on Capitol Hill*" with about 30 Senate Democrats to urge support for the agreement, saying that "*If Congress rejects this good deal, and the U.S. is forced to walk away, Iran will be left with an unconstrained nuclear program with far weaker monitoring arrangements, the current international consensus on sanctions would unravel, and international unity and pressure on Iran would be seriously undermined.*" Former Ambassador Dennis Ross, a longtime American negotiator in the Middle East, wrote that he was not yet convinced by either proponents or opponents of the agreement. Ross wrote that the U.S.'s should be focused on "*deterring the Iranians from cheating*" (e.g., by producing highly enriched uranium) after year fifteen of the agreement. Ross wrote that "*President Obama emphasizes that the agreement is based on verification not trust. But our catching Iran cheating is less important than the price they know they will pay if we catch them. Deterrence needs to apply not just for the life of the deal.*" As part of a deterrence strategy, Ross proposed transferring to Israel the U.S.'s Massive Ordnance Penetrator (MOP) "*bunker buster*" bomb at some point before year fifteen of the agreement.

The Jewish American community was divided on the agreement. On August 19, 2015, leaders of the Reform Jewish movement, the largest Jewish denomination in the U.S., issued a lengthy public statement expressed a neutral position on the agreement statement expressed a neutral position on the agreement.

The statement, signed by the leaders of the Union for Reform Judaism, Central Conference of American Rabbis, Religious Action Center of Reform Judaism and Association of Reform Zionists of America, reflected what Rabbi Rick Jacobs, president of the URJ, called "deep divisions within the movement." On August 20, 2015, a group of 26 prominent current and foreign American Jewish communal leaders published a full-page ad in the New York Times with a statement backing the agreement; signers included three former chairs of the Conference of Presidents of Major American Jewish Organizations as well as former AIPAC executive director Tom Dine. Separately, a group of 340 rabbis organized by Ameinu issued a public letter to Congress on August 17, 2015, in support of the agreement, saying: "*We, along with many other Jewish leaders, fully support this historic nuclear accord.*" The signers were mostly Reform rabbis, but included at least 50 rabbis from the Conservative movement and at least one Orthodox rabbi. Prominent rabbis who signed this letter included Sharon Brous, Burton Visotzky, Nina Beth Cardin, Lawrence Kushner, Sharon Kleinbaum, and Amy Eilberg. Conversely, a group of 900 rabbis signed an open letter written by Kalman Topp and Yonah Bookstein in late August, calling upon Congress to reject the agreement. The Orthodox Union and American Jewish Committee also announced opposition to the agreement.

The Roman Catholic Church expressed support for the agreement. In a July 14, 2015 letter to Congress, Bishop Oscar Cantú, chairman of the Committee on International Justice and Peace of the United States Conference of Catholic Bishops, stated that the JCPOA was "*a momentous agreement*" which "signals progress in global nuclear non-proliferation." Cantú wrote that Bishops in U.S. "*will continue to urge Congress to endorse the result of these intense negotiations because the alternative leads toward armed conflict, an outcome of profound concern to the Church.*" The Vatican also endorsed the deal and issued a statement saying "*We hope that the full implementation of [the nuclear deal] will ensure *the peaceful nature of Iran's nuclear programme under the [Non-Proliferation Treaty] and will be a definitive step toward greater stability and security in the region,*" According to Archbishop Paul Gallagher, (the Vatican's foreign minister, said in a statement delivered at the International Atomic Energy Association in Vienna) "*The way to resolve disputes and difficulties should always be that of dialogue and negotiations.*"

On August 25, 2015, a group of 53 Christian faith leaders from a variety of denominations sent a message to Congress urging them to support the agreement. The Christian leaders wrote: "*This is a moment to remember the wisdom of Jesus who proclaimed from the Sermon on the Mount, 'Blessed are the peacemakers, for they shall be called children of God' (Matthew 5:9). ... There is no question we are all better off with this deal than without it.*" The letter was v coordinated by a Quaker group, the Friends Committee on National Legislation. Signatories to the letter included Jim Wallis of Sojourners; John C. Dorhauer, general minister and president of the United Church of Christ; Shane Claiborne; Adam Estle of Evangelicals for Middle East Understanding; Archbishop Vicken Aykazian of the Armenian Orthodox Church; A. Roy Medley, the head of American Baptist Churches USA; the Reverend Paula Clayton Dempsey of the Alliance of Baptists, senior pastor Joel C. Hunter of Northland, A Church Distributed; and Sister Simone Campbell, a leader of the Catholic "Nuns on the Bus" campaigns.

On Sept 3, a letter signed by fifty-nine people with arms control expertise was sent to President Obama criticizing the JCPOA as "*unverifiable.*" They said in the letter, "*Guided by our experience with U.S. and foreign nuclear weapons programs – as well as with the history and practice of arms control, nonproliferation, and intelligence matters, we judge the current JCPOA to be a very bad deal indeed.*" The letter, which included a 14-page analysis of the JCPOA, was drafted by former State Department Assistant Secretary for Verification and Compliance Paula DeSutter and former ACDA assistant director Henry Cooper. It was also signed by ACDA former deputy director Stephen Read Hanmer, former assistant director for verification and intelligence Manfred Eimer, former assistant director for nonproliferation Kathleen Bailey and former arms control policy advisor Brig. Gen. Larry Grundhauser, and C. Paul Robinson, the former president and director of Sandia National Laboratories, head of the nuclear weapons and national security programs at Los Alamos National Laboratory, and chief negotiator at the U.S./Soviet Union nuclear testing talks. Other signers included former CIA director James Woolsey, former national security advisor Robert McFarlane, former undersecretary of state for arms control and international security and ambassador to the UN John Bolton, and former deputy undersecretary of defense for intelligence, Lt. Gen. William "Jerry" Boykin, and former assistant secretary of energy for defense programs Troy Wade.

CHAPTER NINE

Congressional Committee Hearings

A hearing on the JCPOA before the Senate Foreign Relations Committee took place on July 23, 2015. Secretary of State Kerry, Treasury Secretary Jack Lew and Energy Secretary Moniz testified. Republican Senator Bob Corker of Tennessee, the committee chairman, said in his opening statement that when the talks began the goal was to dismantle the Iranian nuclear program, whereas the achieved agreement codified "*the industrialization of their nuclear program.*" Corker, addressing Secretary of State Kerry, said, "*I believe you've been fleeced and, what you've really done here is you have turned Iran from being a pariah to now Congress, Congress being a pariah.*" Corker asserted that a new threshold in U.S. foreign policy was crossed and the agreement would "*enable a state sponsor of terror to obtain sophisticated, industrial nuclear development program that has, as we know, only one real practical need.*" The committee's ranking Democratic member, Senator Benjamin Cardin of Maryland, said he had many questions and his hope was that the answers will cause a debate "*in Congress and the American people.*" Corker and Cardin sent a letter to Obama saying the bilateral IAEA-Iran document should be available for Congress to review. At the hearing Kerry, Lew, and Moniz were unequivocal in their statements that the accord was the best that could be achieved and that without it, the international sanctions regime would collapse.

Kerry warned that if the United States would be on our own if it were to walk away from a multi-lateral agreement alongside the five global powers. Kerry stated that the belief that *"some sort of unicorn arrangement involving Iran's complete capitulation" could be achieved was "a fantasy, plain and simple."* The Washington Post reported that "*Moniz emerged as the calm center of the proceedings, beginning his interjections with recitations of what he described as 'facts,' and mildly observing that Republican characterizations were 'incorrect.'*" Kerry, Lew, and Moniz faced uniform animus of *Republicans* at the hearing, with Republican senators giving "*long and often scathing speeches denouncing what they described as fatally flawed agreement and accusing the administration of dangerous naivete*" and showing "*little interest in responses*" from the three cabinet secretaries. Washington Post reported on twelve issues related to the agreement over which the two sides disagreed at the hearing.

On July 28, Kerry, Moniz, and Lew testified before the House Committee on Foreign Affairs. Committee chairman Ed Royce, Republican of California, said in his opening statement that "*we are being asked to consider an agreement that gives Iran permanent sanctions relief for temporary nuclear restrictions.*" The committee's ranking member, Representative Eliot Engel, Democrat of New York, said he has "serious questions and concerns" about the agreement. Kerry, Lew, and Moniz spent four hours testifying before the committee. At the hearing, Kerry stated that if Congress killed the deal, "*You'll not only be giving Iran a free pass to double the pace of its uranium enrichment, to build a heavy-water reactor, to install new and more efficient centrifuges, but they will do it all without the unprecedented inspection and transparency measures that we have secured. Everything that we have tried to prevent will now happen.*"

On July 29, Secretary of Defense Ashton Carter, General Martin Dempsey, the chairman of the Joint Chiefs of Staff, Kerry, Moniz, and Lew appeared before the Senate Armed Services

Committee in a three-hour hearing. Carter and Dempsey had been invited to testify by Republican Senator John McCain of Arizona, the chairman of the committee; Kerry, Moniz, and Lew attended the hearing at the invitation of the Pentagon. In his opening statement, McCain said that if this agreement failed and U.S. armed forces were called to take action against Iran, they "*could be at greater risk because of this agreement.*" He also asserted that the agreement may lead American allies and partners to fateful decisions and result in "*growing regional security competition, new arms races, nuclear proliferation, and possibly conflict.*" The committee's ranking Democratic member, Senator Jack Reed of Rhode Island, said Congress had an obligation "*to independently validate that the agreement will meet our common goal of stopping Iran from acquiring a nuclear weapon*" and stated that "*the agreement, no matter your position on it, is historic and, if implemented scrupulously, could serve as a strategic inflection point in the world's relations with Iran, for international non-proliferation efforts, and for the political and security dynamics in the Middle East.*" Carter said the agreement prevented Iran from "*getting a nuclear weapon in a comprehensive and verifiable way.*" He assured the committee that the deal would not limit the U.S. to respond with military force if needed. In response to a question from McCain, Carter said he had "*no reason to foresee*" that the agreement would cause Iran's threatening behavior to change more broadly, stating "*That is why it's important that Iran not have a nuclear weapon.*" Dempsey offered what he described as a "*pragmatic*" view. He neither praised nor criticized the deal, but did testify that the agreement reduced the chances of a near-term military conflict between the U.S. and Iran. Dempsey said that the agreement works to keep Iran from developing nuclear weapons, but does not address other concerns about Iran's malign activities in the region, ranging from "*ballistic missile technology to weapons trafficking, to ... malicious activity in cyberspace.*" Dempsey testified that "*Ultimately, time and Iranian behavior will determine if the nuclear agreement is effective and sustainable"* and stated that he would continue to provide military options to the president. Senator Joni Ernst expressed disagreement with President Obama who stated that the choice was the Iran nuclear deal or war. When General Martin Dempsey testified that the U.S. had *"a range of options"* and he presented them to the president, Ernst said: *"it's imperative everybody on the panel understand that there are other options available."*

Under the JCPOA, Iran must submit a full report on its nuclear history before it can receive any sanctions relief. The IAEA has confidential technical arrangements with many countries as a matter of standard operating procedure. *"Republican lawmakers refer to these agreements as 'secret side deals' and claim that the JCPOA hinges on a set of agreements no one in the administration has actually seen."* Senator Tom Cotton of Arkansas, a Republican opponent of the agreement, said that Kerry had *"acted like Pontius Pilate and washed his hands, kicked it to the IAEA, knowing Congress would not get this information unless someone went out to* **find** *it."*

On August 5, Yukiya Amano, director general of the IAEA, spoke with members of the Senate Foreign Relations Committee in a closed briefing about two IAEA documents: an agreement on inspection protocols with Iran and an agreement with Iran regarding Iranian disclosure of its previous nuclear activity (known as Possible Military Dimensions). Following this briefing with Amano, Republican Senator Bob Corker, the committee chairman, told reporters: *"The majority of members here left with far more questions than they had before the meeting took place"* and *"We cannot get him to even confirm that we will have physical access* **inside** *of Parchin."* The committee's ranking Democratic member, Senator Benjamin Cardin told reporters: *"I thought today was helpful, but it was not a substitute for seeing the document."* State Department spokesman John Kirby responded that *"There's no secret deals between Iran and the IAEA that the P5+1 has not* *been briefed on in detail"* and stated *"These kinds of technical arrangements with the IAEA are a matter of standard practice, that they're not released publicly or to other states, but our experts are familiar and comfortable with the contents, which we would be happy to discuss with Congress in a classified setting."* The Center for Arms Control and Non-Proliferation wrote that: *"The arrangement specifies procedural information regarding how the IAEA will conduct its investigation into Iran's past nuclear history, including mentioning the names of informants who will be interviewed. Releasing this information would place those informants, and the information they hold, at risk."* Mark Hibbs of the Nuclear Policy Program at the Carnegie Endowment for International Peace and Thomas Shea, a former IAEA safeguards official and former head of Defense Nuclear Nonproliferation Programs at the Pacific Northwest National Laboratory, wrote that the charges of a *"secret side deal"* made by opponents of the agreement were a *"manufactured controversy."* Hibbs and Shea noted: *"The IAEA has safeguards agreement with 180 countries. All have similar information protection provisions. Without these, governments would not open their nuclear programs for multilateral oversight. So IAEA Director General Yukiya Amano was acting by the book on August 5 when he told members of Congress that he couldn't share with them the details of [the] verification protocol the IAEA had negotiated with Iran as part of a bilateral 'roadmap."*

David Albright, founder and president of the Institute for Science and International Security and a former IAEA nuclear inspector, stated that the demands for greater transparency regarding the agreement between Iran and IAEA *"aren't unreasonable"* and that *"Iran is a big screamer for more confidentiality. Nonetheless, if the IAEA wanted to make it more open, it could."* Albright also proposed that the U.S. *"should clearly and publicly confirm, and Congress should support with legislation, that if Iran does not address the IAEA's concerns about the past military dimensions of its nuclear programs, U.S. sanctions will not be lifted."*

CHAPTER TEN

US Congressional Support and Opposition on the Deal

Republican leaders vowed to attempt to kill the agreement as soon as it was released, even before classified sections were made available to Congress, Republican lawmakers raced to send out news releases criticizing it. According to the Washington Post, "*most congressional Republicans remained deeply skeptical, some openly scornful, of the prospect of relieving economic sanctions while leaving any Iranian uranium-enrichment capability intact.*" Senate Majority Leader Mitch McConnell, Republican of Kentucky, said the deal "*appears to fall well short of the goal we all thought was trying to be achieved, which was that Iran would not be a nuclear state.*" A New York Times news analysis stated that Republican opposition to the agreement "*seems born of genuine distaste for the deal's details, inherent distrust of President Obama, intense loyalty to Israel and an expansive view of the role that sanctions have played beyond preventing Iran's nuclear abilities.*" The Washington Post identified twelve issues related to the agreement on which the two sides disagreed, including the efficacy of inspections at undeclared sites; the effectiveness of the snapback sanctions; the significance of limits on enrichment; the significance of IAEA side agreements; the effectiveness of inspections of military sites; the consequences of walking away from an agreement; and the effects of lifting sanctions. One area of disagreement between supporters and opponents of the JCPOA is the consequences of walking away from *an* agreement, and whether renegotiation of the agreement is a realistic option.

Senator Chuck Schumer, Democrat of New York an opponent of the agreement, called for the U.S. government to keep sanctions in place, strengthen them, and *"pursue the hard-trodden path of diplomacy once more, difficult as it may be."* Senator Bob Corker, Republican of Tennessee, said that he believed that it was *"hyperbole"* to say that the agreement was the only alternative to *war*. President Obama, by contrast, argued that renegotiation of the deal is unrealistic, stating in his American University speech that *"the notion that there is a better deal to be had relies on vague promises of toughness"* and stated that *"Those making this argument are either ignorant of Iranian society, or they are not being straight with the American people. Neither the Iranian government, or the Iranian opposition or the Iranian people would agree to what they would view as a total surrender of their sovereignty."* Obama also argued that *"those who say we can just walk away from this deal and maintain sanctions are selling a fantasy. Instead of strengthening our position, as some have suggested, Congress' rejection would almost certainly result in multi-lateral sanctions unraveling, because our closest allies in Europe or in Asia, much less China or Russia, certainly are not going to enforce existing sanctions for another five, 10, 15 years according to the dictates of the U.S. Congress because their willingness to support sanctions in the first place was based on Iran ending its pursuit of nuclear weapons. It was not based on the belief that Iran cannot have peaceful nuclear power."* Secretary of State Kerry echoed these remarks, saying in July 2015 that *"the idea of a better deal, or some sort of unicorn arrangement involving Iran's complete capitulation is a fantasy, plain and simple, and our intelligence community will tell you that."* Senator Al Franken, Democrat of Minnesota, a supporter of the agreement wrote: *"Some say that, should the Senate reject this agreement, we would be in position to negotiate a "better" one. But I've spoken to representatives of the five nations that helped broker the deal, and they agree that this simply wouldn't be the case."*

On July 28, 2015, Representative Sander M. Levin, Democrat of Michigan, the longest-serving Jewish member now in Congress, announced in a lengthy statement that he would support the JCPOA, saying that *"the agreement is the best way"* to stop Iran *from obtaining a nuclear weapon and that a rejection of the agreement would lead the international sanctions regime to "quickly fall apart," as "sanctions likely would not be continued even by our closest allies, and the U.S. would be isolated trying to enforce our unilateral sanctions as to Iran's banking and oil sectors."* A key figure in the congressional review process was Senator Benjamin Cardin of Maryland, a Democrat who is the ranking member of the Senate Foreign Relations Committee. Cardin took a phone call from Israeli Prime Minister Netanyahu opposing the agreement and participated in a private 90-minute session with Energy Secretary Moniz supporting the agreement. On July 21, Cardin said that if the agreement is implemented, the U.S. should increase military aid to Israel and friendly Gulf states.

On August 4, 2015, three key and closely watched Senate Democrats—Tim Kaine of Virginia (a Foreign Relations Committee member), Barbara Boxer of California (also a Foreign Relations Committee member), and Bill Nelson of Florida—announced their support for the agreement. In a floor speech that day, Kaine said that the agreement is *"far preferable to any other alternative, including war"* and that *"America has honored its best traditions and shown that patient diplomacy can achieve what isolation and hostility cannot."* In a similar floor speech the same day, Nelson said that: *"I am convinced [that the agreement] will stop Iran from developing a nuclear weapon for at least the next 10 to 15 years. No other available alternative accomplishes this vital objective"* and *"If the U.S. walks away from this multinational agreement, I believe we would find ourselves alone in the world with little credibility."*

Conversely, another closely watched senator, Chuck Schumer of New York, announced his opposition to the agreement on August 6, writing that "*there is a strong case that we are better off without an agreement than with one*" according to an Associated Press report, the classified assessment of the United States Intelligence Community on the agreement concludes that because Iran will be required by the agreement to provide international inspectors with "*unprecedented volume of information about nearly every aspect of its existing nuclear program*," Iran's ability to conceal a covert weapons program will be diminished. In an August 13 letter to colleagues, ten current and former Democratic members of the House Select Committee on Intelligence (including House Minority Leader Nancy Pelosi and Intelligence Committee ranking member Adam Schiff) referred to this assessment as a reason to support the agreement, writing that "*We are confident that this monitoring and the highly intrusive inspections provided for in the agreement – along with our own intelligence capabilities – make it nearly impossible for Iran to develop a covert enrichment effort without detection.*" The ten members also wrote "*You need not take our word for it*" and referred members to the classified assessment itself, which is located in an office in the Capitol basement and is available for members of Congress to read.

US Congressional Votes

A resolution of disapproval was initially expected to pass both the House and Senate, meaning that the real challenge for the White House is whether they can marshal enough Democrats to sustain the veto. Two-thirds of both houses (the House of Representatives and the Senate) are required to override a veto, meaning that one-third of either house (146 votes in the House, or 34 in the Senate) could sustain (uphold) President Obama's veto of a resolution of disapproval.

By early September 2015, 34 Senators had publicly

confirmed support for the deal, a crucial threshold because it ensured that the Senate could sustain (i.e., uphold) any veto of a resolution of disapproval. Senator Barbara Mikulski of Maryland announced support on September 2, a day after Chris Coons of Delaware and Bob Casey, Jr. of Pennsylvania also announced support, reaching 34 votes and assuring that an eventual disapproval resolution passed in the Senate could not override an Obama veto. By the following day, 38 Democratic senators supported the deal, 3 were opposed, and 5 were still undecided.

By September 8, all senators had made a commitment on the agreement, with 42 in support (40 Democrats and two independents) and 58 opposed (54 Republicans and four Democrats).The apparent success of a strategy to marshal congressional support for the deal, linked to a carefully-orchestrated rollout of endorsements (although Democratic Senate minority whip Richard Durbin and other officials disputed the suggestion of coordination was attributed to lessons learned by the White House and congressional Democrats during struggles in previous summers with Republicans, in particular, over Obama's health care legislation. An August 2015 meeting at which top diplomats from England, Russia, China, Germany, and France told 10 undecided Democratic senators they had no intention of returning to the negotiating table was reported to be particularly crucial.

"They were clear and strong that we will not join you in re-imposing sanctions", Senator Coons said.

On August 20, 2015, House Minority Leader Nancy Pelosi said that House Democrats had the votes to uphold a veto of a resolution of disapproval. To sustain a veto, Pelosi would need to hold only 145 of the 188 House Democrats; by August 20, about 60 House Democrats had publicly declared their support for the final agreement, and about 12 had publicly declared their opposition. In May 2015, before the final agreement was announced, 151 House Democrats signed in support for the broad outlines in the April framework agreement; none of those signatories announced opposition to the final agreement.

It was originally expected that the House would vote on a formal resolution of disapproval introduced by Representative Ed Royce, Republican of California (the chair of the House Foreign Affairs Committee). As the Senate moved toward a vote on a resolution of disapproval, House leadership (under Republican control) planned to vote on a similar resolution of disapproval. However, conservative Republicans revolted in protest as the chamber's right flank wanted tougher action from its leader and the House Republican leadership (under Speaker John Boehner) planned to vote instead chose to bring a resolution of approval to the floor as a way to effectively force Democrats who had voiced support for the president to formally register such endorsement. On September 11, 2015, the resolution failed, as expected, on a 162-269 vote; 244 Republicans and 25 Democrats voted no, while 162 Democrats and no Republicans voted yes. On the same day, House Republicans held two additional votes, one on a resolution claiming that the Obama administration had failed to meet the requirements of a congressional review period on the deal and another resolution which would prevent the U.S. from lifting any sanctions. The former resolution passed on a party-line vote, with all Republicans in favor and all Democrats opposed; the latter resolution passed on nearly a party-line vote, with all Republicans and two Democrats in favor and every other Democrat opposed. The House action against the resolution was a symbolic vote that will have no consequence for the implementation of the deal, and the two anti-agreement measures passed by the House were seen as unlikely to even reach Obama's desk.

On the 17th of September 2015 (being the deadline for the US Congress to vote for or against the Deal) the measure to block the Iran nuclear deal in the Senate failed to reach the 60 votes it need to override a filibuster. In a final effort to derail the Iran nuclear deal Senate Republicans on that day failed to get enough vote on an amendment that would have required Iran to recognize Israel and release Americans held in Iran before getting sanctions relief from the United States. The amendment, which was considered on the last day Congress by law can act to scuttle the deal, needed 60 votes to pass but failed 53-45. The toughly worded and politically sensitive amendment was designed to pressure Democrats   (most of whom support the Iran deal) to choose between the implementation of the agreement and their commitment to Israel and Americans held in Iran. "*The administration attempted to negotiate this deal with the singular focus of ending Iran's nuclear program,*" said Senate Majority Leader Mitch McConnell before the vote, complaining that "*myopia*" led the White House to ignore the needs of Israel and the prisoners. "*We can say it has to be corrected before sanctions are lifted and billions more flow into Iranian coffers to use for terrorism.*" But Democrats said the effort was a "*cynical show vote,*" in the words of Senate Democratic Leader Harry Reid. "*The issue has been decided,*" **Reid said.** "*But instead of focusing on the critical issue of funding our government, Sen. McConnell has decided to spend the entire week on something that's already been decided, twice.*"

Three of the four Democratic senators who came out against the Iran deal itself voted against this amendment. Only Sen. Joe Manchin of West Virginia voted with the Republicans. Before the vote, McConnell drew complaints from Arizona Republican Sen. Jeff Flake, an opponent of the deal who nevertheless said the leader's tactic of repeated failed procedural votes was "*misguided.*" "*There is not value to our allies to see there is a split here in Congress or between Congress and the executive on this issue,*" he said. In the end, the final outcome of the deal was largely inevitable. It never seemed likely that Republicans would be able to persuade 13 Democrats in the Senate and 44 Democrats in the House to vote against the deal, and even less likely that they would be able to persuade that many to agree to override a Presidential veto on such an important high-stakes issue. Additionally, while there has been some complaint that the deal should have been submitted to the

Senate as a treaty, which would have required 67 votes for ratification, there seems to ample historical and legal evidence that the deal is not in fact a treaty, but rather an executive agreement. Under that theory, President Obama theoretically might not have needed to submit the agreement to Congress at all, so the review process granted by the Iran Nuclear Agreement Review Act actually gave Congress more of a say than it otherwise would have.

Following a final failed attempt by Senate Republicans to kill the Iran nuclear agreement on 17th of September 2015 the Oboma Administration moved aggressively toward putting it into effect, naming a new czar to oversee implementation and announcing that President Obama would issue waivers suspending all U.S. nuclear-related sanctions on October 18th 2015. The waivers will not go into effect until what the agreement itself calls "Implementation Day," when the International Atomic Energy Agency certifies that Iran has complied with all of its obligations — including removal of 98 percent of its enriched uranium stockpile, shutting down its underground enrichment facility and rendering inoperative the core of a plutonium-capable reactor.

Secretary of State John F. Kerry appointed a career foreign service officer, Stephen D. Mull, as implementation coordinator among U.S. agencies and negotiating partners, reporting directly to the secretary's office. Before his most recent job as U.S. ambassador to Poland, Mull played a key role in early negotiations with Iran. Under provisions of the agreement, it must be formally adopted by all parties — including the United States, the five other world powers who participated in the negotiations, and Iran — 90 days after the U.N. Security Council approved it in July. That day is Oct 18th 2015. Signing of the waivers in advance — along with steps expected on Oct 18th 2015 by the European Union to prepare to lift its own nuclear-related sanctions — were included in the deal as a demonstration of good faith as Iran begins its dismantlement. U.S. interaction with Iran will be limited as sanctions related to Iranian support for terrorism will remain in effect. The U.S. waivers, which the president must renew every three to six months, can be reversed if Iran fails to comply with the agreement.

CHAPTER ELEVEN

JCPOA Review Period in Iran

The Iranian Reaction on the Deal

On June 21, 2015, the Iranian Parliament (Majlis) decided to form a committee to study the JCPOA and to wait at least 80 days before voting on it. Foreign minister Mohammad Javad Zarif and Atomic Energy Organization of Iran chief Ali Akbar Salehi, defended the deal in Parliament on the same day. In televised remarks made on July 23, 2015, Iranian President Hassan Rouhani rejected domestic criticism of the JCPOA from Iranian hardliners, *"such as the Islamic Revolutionary Guards Corps and its allies,"* which *"have criticized the accord as an invasive affront to the country's sovereignty and a capitulation to foreign adversaries, particularly the United States."* President Rouhani claimed a popular mandate to make an agreement based on his election in 2013 and warned that the alternative was *"an economic Stone Age"* brought on by sanctions which (as the Times described) have *"shriveled oil exports and denied the country access to the global banking system."* On July 26, a two-page, top-secret directive sent to Iranian newspaper editors from Iran's Supreme National Security Council surfaced online. In the document, newspapers are instructed to avoid criticism of the agreement and to avoid giving the impression of *"a rift"* at the highest levels of government. The BBC reported that the document appears to be aimed at constraining criticism of the JCPOA by Iranian hardliners.

On September 3, Iranian supreme leader Khamenei said that the Majlis should make the final decision on the agreement. On the same day, Ali Larijani, the speaker of the parliament, said that he supports the agreement and that: "*The agreement needs to be discussed and needs to be approved by the Iranian parliament. There will be heated discussions and debates.*" Conversely, "*the most militantly authoritarian, conservative, and anti-Western leaders and groups within Iran oppose the deal.*" The anti-agreement coalition in Iran includes former president Ahmadinejad, known for his Holocaust denial and calls for the elimination of Israel; Fereydoon Abbasi (the director of the Iranian nuclear program during Ahmadinejad's term); ex-nuclear negotiator Saeed Jalili; and various conservative clerics and Revolutionary Guard commanders. This group has "*issued blistering attacks on the incompetence of Iran's negotiating team, claiming that negotiators caved on many key issues and were outmaneuvered by more clever and sinister American diplomats.*" Shortly after the US senates democrats vote of approver of the deal in the US congress, Khodabandeh (A renowned political analyst in Iran) said that "*the fact that Senate Democrats could defeat Republicans over the Iran Nuclear accord shows that the US is getting away from the influence of the American Israel Public Affairs Committee*" According to him, "*This defeat shows really what the AIPAC could not do this time, it shows their weakness*" He noted that "*the core policy of the US is getting away from the influence of AIPAC at least as much as it used to be*" However the Iranian President Rouhani said after the Final US congress vote on 17th of September on the deal that he believes the deal will go through when finally reviewed in the Iranian parliament as "*there was no reason to why it wouldn't*".

CHAPTER TWELVE

Economic Benefits of the Deal

With the prospective lifting of some sanctions, the agreement is expected to have a significant impact on both the economy of Iran and global markets. The energy sector is particularly important, with Iran having nearly 10 percent of global oil reserves and 18 percent of natural gas reserves. Millions of barrels of Iranian oil may come onto global markets, lowering the price of crude oil. However, the impact will not be immediate, because Iran will not be able to implement measures that are needed to lift sanctions until the end of 2015. Technology and investment from global integrated oil companies are expected to increase capacity from Iran's oil fields and refineries, which have been in **"disarray"** in recent years, plagued by mismanagement and underinvestment. The economic impact of a partial lifting of sanctions extends beyond the energy sector; the New York Times reported that **"consumer-oriented companies, in particular, could find opportunity in this country with 81 million consumers,"** many of whom are young and prefer Western products. Iran is considered a strong emerging market play by investment and trading firms.

Scientific Benefits

In July 2015, Richard Stone wrote in the journal Science in July 2015 that if the agreement is fully implemented, **"*Iran can expect a rapid expansion of scientific cooperation with Western powers. As its nuclear facilities are repurposed, scientists from*"**

Iran and abroad will team up in areas such as nuclear fusion, astrophysics, and radioisotopes for cancer therapy."

Diplomatic Benefits

In August 2015, the British embassy in Tehran reopened almost four years after it was closed after protesters attacked the embassy in

2011. At a reopening ceremony, Hammond said that since Rouhani's election as president, British-Iranian relations had gone from a *"low   point"* to steady *"step-by-step"* improvement. Hammond said: *"historic nuclear agreement was another milestone, and showed the* power *of diplomacy, conducted in an atmosphere of mutual respect, to solve shared challenges. Re-opening the embassy is the logical next step to build confidence and trust between two great nations."* The BBC's diplomatic correspondent, Jonathan Marcus, reported that the nuclear agreement *"had clearly been decisive in prompting the UK embassy to be reopened,"* stating that British-Iranian *"ties have slowly been warming but it is clearly the successful conclusion of the nuclear accord with Iran that has paved the way for the embassy reopening."*

CHAPTER THIRTEEN

Facts to Note about the Iran Deal

^ The P5+1 are also sometimes referred to as the "E3+3" (for the "EU three" countries (France, the UK, and Germany) plus the three non-EU countries (the U.S., Russia, and China)). Both terms are interchangeable.

^ The meaning of Article IV of the Nuclear Non-proliferation Treaty, and its application to Iran. The U.S. position was unclear before 2006, but after that time the U.S. has taken the position that Iran does not have the right to uranium enrichment because this activity is not specifically cited in the NPT. In testimony before the Senate Foreign Relations Committee in October 2013, Sherman stated that "*the U.S. position that that article IV of the Nuclear Nonproliferation Treaty does not speak about the right of enrichment at all [and] doesn't speak to enrichment, period. It simply says that you have the right to research and development. And many countries such as Japan and Germany have taken that uranium enrichment to be a right. But the United States does not take that position. ... We do not believe there is an inherent right by anyone to enrichment.*" The U.S. officials have also made the additional argument that whatever Iran's rights under the NPT might be, they were superseded by a series of UN Security Council resolutions demanding "*that Iran suspend enrichment and reprocessing activities until 'confidence is restored in the purely peaceful nature of Iran's nuclear program.*" U.S. Secretary of State Kerry has said: "*We do not recognize a right to enrich. It is clear;*

In the nonproliferation treaty, it's very, very (clear) that there is no right to enrich. [The Iranians] have the ability to negotiate it, but they could only gain that capacity to have some enrichment as some countries do, if they live up to the whole set of terms necessary to prove its a peaceful program." In March 2011 testimony before the House Foreign Affairs Committee, then-U.S. Secretary of State Hillary Rodham Clinton expressed a similar position, indicating that Iran should be permitted to enrich uranium under IAEA supervision once the international concerns over its nuclear program are resolved.

^ At the same time that the JCPOA was agreed to, Iran and the IAEA signed a separate document, the Roadmap for Clarification of Past and Present Outstanding Issues. The roadmap includes "the provision by Iran of explanations regarding outstanding issues" and provides *"for technical expert meetings, technical measures and discussions, as well as a separate arrangement regarding the issue of Parchin,"* **an Iranian military research and development site.** *"The specific measures that Iran is committed to take with respect to technical expert meetings and discussions and access to Parchin are contained in two separate documents between Iran and the IAEA that are not public."* On August 19, 2015, the Associated Press reported that an anonymous official had given the AP an unsigned, preliminary draft of one of the confidential bilateral IAEA-Iran agreements. This draft indicated that Iran would be allowed to use its own inspectors to investigate the Parchin site. The AP reported that two anonymous officials had told it that the draft does not differ from the final, confidential agreement between the IAEA and Iran). The AP said that the draft *"diverges from normal procedures."* Several hours after posting the article, the AP removed several details of the story (without issuing a formal retraction), and published another article that noted that *"IAEA staff will monitor Iranian personnel as they inspect the Parchin nuclear site."* The AP restored the contentious details the next morning and said it was standing by its entire story.

It further published the full document it had transcribed. The following day, IAEA Director General Yukiya Amano issued a statement stating: "*I am disturbed by statements suggesting that the IAEA has given responsibility for nuclear inspections to Iran. Such statements misrepresent the way in which we will undertake this important verification work ... the arrangements are technically sound and consistent with our long-established practices. They do not compromise our safeguards standards in any way. The Road-map between Iran and the IAEA is a very robust agreement, with strict timelines, which will help us to clarify past and present outstanding issues regarding Iran's nuclear programme.*" The IAEA did not elaborate on the provisions of the confidential agreement, but the Arms Control Association has noted that under managed access procedures that may be employed the IAEA, the inspected party may take environmental swipe samples at a particular site in the presence of the IAEA inspectors using swabs and containment bags provided by the IAEA to prevent cross contamination. According to former IAEA officials, this is an established procedure. Such swipe samples collected at suspect sites under managed access would likely be divided into six packages: three are taken by the IAEA for analysis at its Seibersdorf Analytical Lab and two to be sent to the IAEA's Network of Analytical Labs (NWAL), which comprises some 16 labs in different countries, and another package to be kept under joint IAEA and Iran seal at the IAEA office in Iran a backup and control sample if re-analysis might be required at a later stage. The process ensures the integrity of the inspection operation and the samples for all parties. Mark Hibbs of the Nuclear Policy Program at the Carnegie Endowment for International Peace and Thomas Shea, a former IAEA safeguards official and head of Defense Nuclear Nonproliferation Programs at the Pacific Northwest National Laboratory described a similar protocol in an article entitled "*No, Iran is not allowed to inspect itself.*" Hibbs and Shea wrote that the claims that Iran would be in charge of inspections at Parchin were "*wholly specious*" and "*unfounded*." Arms control expert Jeffrey Lewis of the Monterey Institute of International Studies stated that the procedures referred to in the AP report were consistent with expert practice: "*There are precedents for just providing photos and videos. When the South Africans disabled their nuclear test shaft, they video-recorded it and sent the IAEA their video. I don't care who takes a swipe sample or who takes a photograph, so long as I know where and when it was taken, with very high confidence, and I know that it hasn't been tampered with.*" Lewis expressed the opinion that "*the point of the leak was to make the IAEA agreement on Parchin sound as bad as possible, and to generate political attention in Washington.*" The position of the U.S. government is different. Secretary of State Kerry stated in a Senate Foreign Relations Committee hearing that "*with respect to the talks, we've been clear from the beginning. We're not negotiating a, quote, 'legally binding plan.' We're negotiating a plan that will have in it a capacity for enforcement.*" (Kerry also said that a future president is, as a practical matter, unlikely to "*turn around and just nullify it*" given the international agreement from the other P5+1 powers. Several legal scholars support this argument. John B. Bellinger III argues: "*The next president will have the legal right under both domestic and international law to scrap the JCPOA and reimpose U.S. nuclear sanctions on Iran.*" Bellinger stated that "*such an action would be inconsistent with political commitments made by the Obama administration and would likely cause a major rift with U.S. allies and Iran to resume its nuclear activities, but that would not constitute a violation of international law, because the JCPOA is not legally binding.*" Orde Kittrie of Arizona State University similarly writes that the JCPOA is a kind of "*nonbinding, unsigned political*" agreement considered "*more flexible than treaties or other legally binding international agreements.*"

The "*vast majority of international agreements*" negotiated by the United States, especially in recent decades, have been executive agreements, rather than treaties. In 2003, the U.S.

Supreme Court held in American Insurance Association v. Garamendi that "*our cases have recognized that the President has authority to make 'executive agreements' with other countries, requiring no ratification by the Senate or approval by Congress, this power having been exercised since the early years of the Republic*." Various opponents of the JCPOA, including David B. Rivkin Jr., Lee A. Casey, and Michael Ramsey criticized the form of the agreement, arguing that it should be considered a treaty rather than an executive agreement. Other commentators disagree; the constitutionality of the executive agreement form of the JCPOA has been defended by Jack Goldsmith, who called arguments for the illegality of the agreement "*weak*," and by John Yoo, who wrote that the executive agreement form of the JCPOA is consistent with the Treaty Clause of the Constitution.

The Iran Nuclear Agreement Review Act of 2015, Pub.L. 114–17 was an amendment to the Atomic Energy Act of 1954. The act was passed by the Senate as S. 615 on May 7, 2015, in a 98-1 vote, and was passed by the House as H.R. 1191 on May 14, 2015, in a 400-25 vote, and was approved by President Obama on May 22, 2015.

Much of the criticism of the deal from opponents in the U.S. Congress and from the Israeli government derives from the fact that slowing and shrinking Iran's nuclear program this way falls well short of the original diplomatic goal, which was to end entirely Iran's ability to enrich uranium—the *'zero enrichment'* goal. Before the JCPOA, there was a preference on the part of the United States and many of its allies for zero enrichment in Iran (indeed, opposition to the spread of any uranium enrichment capability to any additional countries has been long-standing U.S. policy and an important nonproliferation principle), although the potential to discuss with Iran the conditions under which it could continue enrichment is not new and was built into the proposals that the P5+1 have offered Iran since 2006, spanning the George W. Bush and Barack Obama administrations. Some commentators, such as Michael Singh of the Washington Institute for Near East Policy (writing in 2013), argued for a zero enrichment approach: i.e., that no agreement contemplating any enrichment by Iran should be made. This was also the position of Senator Bob Menendez of New Jersey, who introduced the Nuclear Weapons Free Iran Act, a proposed bill (not enacted) which would require that Iran reduce its uranium enrichment to zero before an agreement is made. Other commentators have said that "*zero enrichment*" has long been an implausible goal, including R. Nicholas Burns of Harvard's Belfer Center, the Under Secretary of State for Political Affairs and leading figure on Iranian nuclear matters during the second Bush administration, said that this was implausible given that Iran has 19,000 centrifuges, stating: "*If I could get an ideal solution, or you could, where the Iranians submitted to every demand we had, I would take that. In a real world, you have to make real-world decisions.*" Similarly, Michael A. Levi of the Maurice R. Greenberg Center for Geo-economics Studies at the Council on Foreign Relations argued in the August–September 2011 edition of the journal Survival that "*it is far from clear that zero enrichment is a realistic goal*" and stated that "*the goal of current US policy, even if it is not typically* articulated *this way, is limited enrichment, in which Iran has some non-trivial enrichment capability, but is unable to produce a bomb (or small arsenal) without risking strong international retaliation, including military destruction of its enrichment infrastructure.*" Similar arguments have been advanced by Mark Jansson, adjunct fellow at the Federation of American Scientists who wrote in October 2013 in The National Interest that "*there is nothing clear-eyed or realistic about the demand for zero enrichment*" and "*nor is it technically necessary*" George Perkovich, director of the Nonproliferation Program at the Carnegie Endowment for International Peace (who argued in January 2014 in Foreign Affairs that "*the complete elimination of Iran's nuclear fuel cycle program*" is not "*an achievable goal*" and what is needed is "*not the cessation of Iran's nuclear enrichment but its capacity to create a nuclear weapon quickly"*.

Scholars differ on whether a **"better deal"** from the American point of view is realistic. Stephen M. Walt of Harvard, writing an article entitled *"The Myth of the Better Deal"* in Foreign Policy magazine, argued that the idea of an achievable better deal is *"magical thinking"* that is at odds with the facts and *"ignores Diplomacy 101."* Albert Carnesale of Harvard's Belfer Center wrote that *"there is no real alternative that would serve the interests of the United States and our allies and friends as well as the deal that is now before Congress. A 'better deal' is unachievable; a military solution is unrealistic (and probably would be counterproductive); and an international agreement without U.S. participation is less attractive than an agreement in which the U.S. has a strong voice in resolving of issues that might arise."*

References

"Zarif: We've never claimed nuclear deal only favors Iran". Tehran Times. 22 July 2015.

Joshua Keating, You say P5+1, I say E3+3, Foreign Policy (September 30, 2009).

Jeffrey Lewis, E3/EU+3 or P5+1, Arms Control Wonk (July 13, 2015).

Jonas Schneider & Oliver Thränert, Dual Use: Dealing with Uranium Enrichment, CSS Analyses in Security Policy, No. 151 (April 2014).

Iran nuclear talks: 'Historic' agreement struck, BBC News (July 14, 2015).

Paul K. Kerry, Iran's Nuclear Program: Tehran's Compliance with International Obligations, Congressional; Research Service (June 25, 2015).

"Optimism as Iran nuclear deal framework announced; more work ahead". CNN. 3 April 2015. Retrieved 3 April 2015.

Anne Gearan and Joby Warrick (23 November 2013). "World powers reach nuclear deal with Iran to freeze its nuclear program". The Washington Post. Retrieved 3 April 2015.

"IAEA Head Reports Status of Iran's Nuclear Programme". International Atomic Energy Agency. 20 January 2014. Retrieved 23 February 2014.

Louis Charbonneau and Parisa Hafezi (18 July 2014). "Iran, powers extend talks after missing nuclear deal deadline". Reuters. Retrieved 19 July 2014.

Matthew Lee and George Jahn (24 November 2014). "Iran nuclear talks to be extended until July". Associated Press. Retrieved 24 November 2014.

Pamela Dockins (30 June 2015). "Iran Nuclear Talks Extended Until July 7". Voice of America. Retrieved 30 June 2015.

Paul Richter (7 July 2015). "Iran nuclear talks extended again; Friday new deadline". Los Angeles Times. Retrieved 8 July 2015.

Karen DeYoung & Carol Morello, The path to a final Iran nuclear deal: Long days and short tempers, The Washington Post (15 July 2015).

Jethro Mullen and Nic Robertson, CNN (14 July 2015). "Landmark deal reached on Iran nuclear program". CNN.

William J. Broad, Iran Accord's Complexity Shows Impact of Bipartisan Letter, the New York Times (14 July 2015).

Public Statement on U.S. Policy Toward the Iran Nuclear Negotiations Endorsed by a Bipartisan Group of American Diplomats, Legislators, Policymakers, and Experts, Washington Institute for Near East Policy (24 June 2015).

"Iran nuclear deal: world powers reach historic agreement to lift sanctions". The Guardian. 14 July 2015. Retrieved 14 July 2015.

Kelsey Davenport & Daryl G. Kimball, Would the IAEA Depend on Iran for Nuclear Residue Testing? No., Arms Control Association (July 30, 2015).

Mark Hibbs & Thomas Shea, No, Iran is not allowed to inspect itself, The Hill (August 21, 2015).

Ishaan Tharoor, How the nuclear deal can keep Iran from 'cheating,' according to a former U.N. inspector, The Washington Post (15 July 2015).

Richard Nephew, Based on breakout timelines, the world is better off with the Iran nuclear deal than without it, Brookings Institution (July 17, 2015).

Jackie Northam, Lifting Sanctions Will Release $100 Billion To Iran. Then What?, All Things Considered, NPR (July 16, 2015).

Felicia Schwartz, When Sanctions Lift, Iranian Commander Will Benefit, The Wall Street Journal (15 July 2015).

Kenneth Katzman (August 4, 2015). "Iran Sanctions" (PDF). Congressional Research Service. Retrieved September 5, 2015. The Administration asserts that it would implement the relief using waiver authority (for relevant U.S. statutory sanctions) and administrative action (for those sanctions in force only by executive order).

Kenneth Katzman (August 4, 2015). "Iran Sanctions" (PDF). Congressional Research Service. Retrieved September 5, 2015. The U.S. sanctions that are to be suspended are primarily those that sanction foreign entities and countries for conducting specified transactions with Iran (so called "secondary sanctions"). U.S. sanctions that generally prohibit U.S. firms from conducting transactions with Iran are not being altered under the JCPA.

Reuters, Iran's Zarif, EU say nuclear deal is new chapter of hope (16 July 2015).

Ray Locker, First take: Obama's winning streak continues with Iran deal, USA Today (14 July 2015).

Paul Lewis, Obama vows to veto any Republican attempt to derail Iran nuclear deal, The Guardian (14 July 2015).

Carrie Dann, 2016 Republican Candidates Slam Iran Nuke Deal, NBC News (14 July 2015).

Tom LoBianco & Sophie Tatum, GOP 2016 hopefuls slam Iran nuclear deal, CNN (14 July 2015).

Adam Wollner, How the 2016 Presidential Candidates Are Reacting to the Iran Deal, National Journal (14 July 2015).

Lawder, David (14 July 2015). Trott, Bill, ed. "U.S. House Speaker Boehner says Iran accord looks like a 'bad deal'". Retrieved 15 July 2015.

.

Remarks by the President on the Iran Nuclear Deal, American University, Washington, D.C., White House Office of the Press Secretary (August 5, 2015). Another transcript of this speech was also printed by the Washington Post.

Chuck Schumer (7 August 2015). "My Position on the Iran Deal". Medium. Retrieved 7 August 2015.

Eliza Collins, President Obama stands by comments linking Republicans to Iranian hard-liners, Politico (August 10, 2015).

Joint Statement of Iranian-American Organizations on the U.S.-Iran Nuclear Deal, National Iranian American Council (July 29, 2015).

NIAC Applauds Historic Iran Deal, National Iranian American Council (July 14, 2015).

Nahal Toosi, Scholars: Iran deal will stabilize Mideast: The latest letter on the Iran nuclear deal focuses on potential benefits to the volatile region, Politico (August 27, 2015). See also full text of letter.

Felicia Schwartz, Pro-Israel Groups in U.S. Square Off Over Iran Nuke Deal, Wall Street Journal (July 16, 2015).

Alexander Bolton, New group backed by AIPAC targets deal, The Hill (July 17, 2015).

Byron Tau, AIPAC Funds Ads Opposing Iran Nuclear Deal, Wall Street Journal (July 17, 2015).

Ailsa Chang, Lobbyists Spending Millions to Sway the Undecided on Iran Deal, NPR (August 6, 2015).

John Bresnahan & Anna Palmer, Iran deal foes spend big, get little so far, Politico (August 4, 2015).

Jacob Kornbluh, J Street launches multimillion dollar campaign in support of Iran nuclear deal, Haaretz (July 16, 2015).

Gus Burns, First look at $2 million J-Street ad campaign in support of Iran nuclear deal, MLive.com (August 4, 2015).

John Fritze, J Street runs ads in Maryland supporting Iran deal, Baltimore Sun (August 4, 2015).

Citizens for a Nuclear Free Iran (CNFI) Launches Third National TV Ad (press release), United Against Nuclear Iran (August 20, 2015).

Michael R. Gordon, Head of Group Opposing Iran Accord Quits Post, Saying He Backs Deal, New York Times (August 11, 2015).

Will Bredderman, Religious Jewish Pols Bash Manhattan Congressman Over Iran Deal Support, Observer (August 21, 2015).

Allison Kaplan Sommer, Ad Nauseum: How Supporters and Opponents Are Trying to Sell the Iranian Nuclear Deal, Haaretz (August 26, 2015).

Peter Waldman, How Freelance Diplomacy Bankrolled by Rockefellers Has Paved the Way for an Iran Deal, Bloomberg Politics (July 2, 2015).

Julian Hattem, More than 100 ex-US ambassadors pledge backing for Iran deal, The Hill (July 17, 2015).

Letter to the President from over 100 former American Ambassadors on the Joint Comprehensive Plan of Action on Iran's Nuclear Program (July 17, 2015).

James Fallows, A Guide to the Iran Nuclear Deal's Supporters and Opponents, The Atlantic (July 28, 2015).

Letter to Congressional Leadership from Former Under Secretaries of State and former American Ambassadors to Israel on the Joint Comprehensive Plan of Action (July 27, 2015).

Statement by 60 National Security Leaders on the Announcement of a Joint Comprehensive Plan of Action, The Iran Project (July 20, 2015).

Joe Cirincione, 60 of America's Top National Security Leaders Endorse Iran Deal, Huffington Post (July 21, 2015).

William J. Broad, 29 U.S. Scientists Praise Iran Nuclear Deal in Letter to Obama, New York Times (August 8, 2015).

Scientists' Letter to Obama on Iran Nuclear Deal (August 8, 2015), reprinted by the New York Times.

Karen DeYoung, Dozens of retired generals, admirals back Iran nuclear deal, Washington Post (August 11, 2015).

An open letter from retired generals and admirals on the Iran nuclear deal (letter released August 11, 2015), reprinted by the Washington Post.

Emma-Jo Morris, More Than 200 Retired Generals & Admirals Sign Letter Opposing the Iran Deal, IranTruth.org (August 26, 2015, subsequently updated).

Morello, Carol (August 26, 2015). "Retired generals and admirals urge Congress to reject Iran nuclear deal". Washington Post.

"Read: An open letter from retired generals and admirals opposing the Iran nuclear deal".

Mark Thompson, Retired Generals Wage Letter War Over Iran Nuclear Deal Vote, Time (August 27, 2015).

The Comprehensive P5+1 Nuclear Agreement With Iran: A Net-Plus for Nonproliferation: Statement from Nuclear Nonproliferation Specialists, Arms Control Association (August 17, 2015).

American Jewish Committee Opposes Iran Nuclear Deal, Jewish Telegraph Agency (August 5, 2015).

Vinnie Rotondaro, Signs of 'seamless garment' in Catholic support for Iran nuke deal, National Catholic Reporter (August 13, 2015).

Bishop Cantú Welcomes Iran Nuclear Deal, Urges Congress To Endorse Result of Negotiations, United States Conference of Catholic Bishops (July 14, 2015).

Anne K Walters (30 July 2015). "US defence chief tells Congress military options remain against Iran". Deutsche Presse-Agentur. Retrieved 10 August 2015.

Martin Matishak, Obama officials deny 'secret deals' in Iran nuclear pact, The Hill (July 22, 2015).

Associated Press, IAEA can't give Congress its nuke document with Iran, Amano says (August 6, 2015).

Michael Mathes (5 August 2015). "IAEA chief fails to reassure US senators on Iran deal". Agence France-Presse. Retrieved 11 August 2015.

Stephen M. Walt, The Myth of a Better Deal, Foreign Policy (August 10, 2015).

Albert Carnesale, Deal or No Deal: The Choice Before Congress, National Interest (August 5, 2015) (reprinted by the Harvard Belfer Center for Science and International Affairs).

Robert Satloff, A Better Deal With Iran Is Possible, The Atlantic (August 13, 2015).

Levin Statement on the Iran Nuclear Agreement (July 28, 2015).

Melissa Nann Burke & David Shepardson, Rep. Levin backs Iran nuke agreement; others undecided, Detroit News (July 28, 2015).

Mike DeBonis, Three Senate Democrats came off of the fence to support the Iran deal, Washington Post (August 4, 2015).

Senator Bill Nelson on Iran Nuclear Agreement, C-SPAN (August 4, 2015).

Zac Anderson, Nelson supports Iran nuclear deal, Herald-Tribune (August 4, 2011).

Alex Leary, Bill Nelson announces support for Iran nuclear deal, Tampa Bay Times (August 4, 2015).

Paul Kane, Sen. Charles Schumer announces opposition to nuclear pact with Iran, Washington Post (August 6, 2015).

Ken Dilanian, US officials say they can tell if Iran is cheating on deal, Associated Press (August 12, 2015).

Karoun Demirjian, House Dems pounce on intel assessment of Iran deal, Washington Post (August 13, 2015).

Current and Former House Intelligence Committee Members Urge Colleagues to Review Intelligence Community Assessments of Iran Nuclear Deal, United States House Permanent Select Committee on Intelligence Democratic Office (August 13, 2015).

Lauren French, GOP can disapprove Iran deal, but veto remains a hurdle, Politico (August 3, 2015).

Julie Hirschfeld Davis, Lobbying Fight Over Iran Nuclear Deal Centers on Democrats, New York Times (August 17, 2015).

Amber Phillips, Whip count: Where the Senate stands on the Iran deal, Washington Post (August 5, 2015).

Lauren French, Liberals poised to give Barack Obama a win on Iran, Politico (August 13, 2015).

Amber Phillips, Obama's Iran deal nears a major symbolic victory, Washington Post (September 8, 2015).

Booker, Brakkton (September 2, 2015). "Obama Secures Enough Support For Iran Deal In Congress". NPR. Retrieved September 2, 2015.

"A Look at Where Senate Democrats Stand on the Iran Deal". The New York Times. September 3, 2015. Retrieved September 6, 2015.

DeBonis, Mike (September 11, 2015). "How Sen. Durbin spent his summer saving the Iran deal". Washington Post. Retrieved September 12, 2015.

Hulse, Karl; Herszenhorn, David M. (September 2, 2015). "Coordinated Strategy Brings Obama Victory on Iran Nuclear Deal". The New York Times. Retrieved September 6, 2015.

Sabrina Siddiqui, Congress does not have votes to block Iran deal, says Nancy Pelosi, The Guardian (August 20, 2015).

Ryan Grim & Laura Barron-Lopez, Nancy Pelosi May Save The Iran Negotiations For Obama, Huffington Post (April 14, 2015).

Erica Werner, Pelosi: House Democrats will sustain Obama veto on Iran deal, Associated Press (August 20, 2015).

Kristina Peterson, GOP Leaders Back Vote to Disapprove of Iran Nuclear Deal Wall Street Journal (August 4, 2015).

Emma Dumain, Royce, Boehner Set Stage for House Disapproval of Iran Deal, Roll Call (August 4, 2015).

Sabrina Siddiqui, House rejects Obama's nuclear accord with Iran in symbolic vote, Guardian (September 12, 2015).

Final Vote Results for Roll Call 493 (September 11, 2015), Office of the Clerk of the United States House of Representatives.

Lauren French, House GOP disapproves of Iran deal in symbolic vote, Politico (September 11, 2015).

Final Vote Results for Roll Call 492 and Final Vote Results for Roll Call 494 (September 11, 2015), Office of the Clerk of the United States House of Representatives.

Karoun Demirjian & Kelsey Snell, House conservatives may end up in court to kill Iran deal, Washington Post (September 10, 2015).

Thomas Erdbrink, Iran Lawmakers to Wait 80 Days Before Voting on Nuclear Deal, New York Times (July 21, 2015).

Thomas Erdbrink & Rock Gladstone, Iran's President Defends Nuclear Deal in Blunt Remarks, New York Times (July 23, 2015).

Kasra Naji, Iran nuclear: Media ordered to be positive about deal, BBC Persian (July 26, 2015).

Jay Solomon, Iran Leaders Say Parliament Will Have Final Say on Fate of Nuclear Deal, Wall Street Journal (September 3, 2015).

Abbas Milani & Michael McFaul, What the Iran-Deal Debate Is Like in Iran, The Atlantic (August 11, 2015).

"Parl. begins 10th session on reviewing JCPOA". Mehr News Agency. September 13, 2015.

Arash Karami (September 8, 2015). "Former Iran deal negotiator slams concessions in nuclear deal". Al-Monitor.

"Iran Tracker". Critical Threats, American Enterprise Institute. Retrieved September 17, 2015.

"Zarif attends Majlis committee on JCPOA". Tehran Times. September 15, 2015. TTime-249411.

Tara Kangarlou, Tehran's debate over nuclear pact mirrors Washington's, Al-Jazeera (August 13, 2015).

Iranian Dissidents Against the Iran Deal, Daily Beast (August 14, 2015).

Dennis Ross and David Petraeus (25 August 2015). "How to put some teeth into the nuclear deal with Iran". The Washington Post. Retrieved 28 August 2015.

Robert J. Einhorn (August 2015). "The battleground-issues". Brookings Institution. Retrieved 28 August 2015.

Michael Eisenstadt (29 July 2015). "The Nuclear Deal with Iran: Regional Implications". Washington Institute for Near East Policy. Retrieved 28 August 2015.

Staff writers (18 July 2015). "Ayatollah Ali Khamenei criticises 'arrogance' of the United States following nuclear deal". The Telegraph. Retrieved 24 August 2014.

"Obama's Letter to Congressman Nadler". The New York Times. 20 August 2015. Retrieved 28 August 2015.

Kristina Wong (27 August 2015). "Petraeus still making up his mind on Iran deal". The Hill. Retrieved 28 August 2015.

David E. Sanger and Michael R. Gordon (23 August 2015). "Future Risks of an Iran Nuclear Deal". The New York Times. Retrieved 28 August 2015.

Michael Mandelbaum (30 July 2015). "It's the Deterrence, Stupid". The American Interest. Retrieved 28 August 2015.

Alan Dershowitz (2015). The Case Against the Iran Deal: How Can We Now Stop Iran from Getting Nukes? (Kindle Locations 794-795). RosettaBooks. Kindle Edition. ISBN 9780795347559. See also Excerpt from 'The Case Against the Iran Deal'.

Clifford Krauss, A New Stream of Oil for Iran, but Not Right Away, The New York Times (14 July 2015).

Bill Spindle, Nicole Friedman & Benoît Faucon, Iran Deal Raises Prospect of Fresh Oil Glut, The Wall Street Journal (14 July 2015).

Jason Chow, Peugeot in Talks to Re-Establish Auto Manufacturing in Iran, The Wall Street Journal (15 June 2015).

Richard Stone, In Depth: Nuclear Diplomacy: Iran nuclear deal holds 'goodies' for scientists, Science, Vol. 349 no. 6246 pp. 356-357, doi:10.1126/science.349.6246.356.

British embassy in Tehran reopens four years after closure, BBC News (August 23, 2015).

UK embassy in Tehran to reopen after thaw in British-Iranian relations, BBC News (August 20, 2015).